Lucy Moore works for BRF a[...] responsible for developing the work of Messy Church nationally and internationally—writing, speaking, reflecting and developing Messy projects. She continues to help lead the local Messy Church in her own church, where her husband is the minister.

Before working full-time with Messy Church, Lucy was a member of BRF's Barnabas children's ministry team, offering training for those wanting to bring the Bible to life for children in churches and schools across the UK, and using drama and storytelling to explore the Bible with children herself.

Her books include *Messy Church*, *Messy Crafts*, *The Gospels Unplugged*, *The Lord's Prayer Unplugged* and *Colourful Creation* (all Barnabas) and *All-Age Worship* (BRF, 2010), and she presents the *Messy Church* DVD.

Messy Church is growing! Every month, families who have never set foot in a church before are enjoying Messy Church, and every month more Messy Churches are started all over the UK and worldwide. Messy Church is proving effective in sharing God's good news with families across denominations and church traditions. We estimate that some 100,000 people belong to Messy Churches—and the number is growing all the time. For more information about Messy Church, visit www.messychurch.org.uk.

Messy Church is enabled, resourced and supported by BRF (Bible Reading Fellowship), a Registered Charity, as one of its core ministries. BRF makes Messy Church freely available and derives no direct income from the work that we do to support it in the UK and abroad.

Would you be willing to support this ministry with your prayer and your giving? To find out more, please visit www.messychurch.org.uk/champions.

Barnabas for Children

Barnabas for Children® is a registered word mark and the logo is a registered device mark of The Bible Reading Fellowship.
Messy Church® is a registered word mark and the logo is a registered device mark of The Bible Reading Fellowship.

Text copyright © Lucy Moore 2008
The author asserts the moral right
to be identified as the author of this work

Published by
The Bible Reading Fellowship
15 The Chambers, Vineyard
Abingdon OX14 3FE
United Kingdom
Tel: +44 (0)1865 319700
Email: enquiries@brf.org.uk
Website: www.brf.org.uk
BRF is a Registered Charity

ISBN 978 1 84101 602 3
First published 2008
Reprinted 2009, 2010, 2011
10 9 8 7 6 5 4 3
All rights reserved

Acknowledgments
Unless otherwise stated, scripture quotations are taken from the Contemporary English Version of the Bible published by HarperCollins Publishers, copyright © 1991, 1992, 1995 American Bible Society.

A catalogue record for this book is available from the British Library

Printed in Singapore by Craft Print International

Ideas for discipling a Christ-centred community

Messy CHURCH 2

Lucy Moore

For a group of friends and family whose prolonged breakfasts, sub-Arctic picnics, lardy gike-filled teas and candlelit suppers have created so many memories, and without whom the banquet of life would be so much less flavoursome: Jenny, Mike, Matthew and Duncan Gilbertson, Rex Sweeny, Roo Waters and Kate Griffiths, Brice, Tina and Laurence Avery and, of course, Paul, Arthur and Judith Moore, with much love.

ACKNOWLEDGMENTS

Thank you to our marvellous Messy Church team at St Wilfrid's; Sharon Durant and Martin Gee for all their work on the website; the Barnabas team and the BRF team for wisdom and encouragement; Messy Church teams from all over who have contributed ideas to the book and website; the thinkers at The Sheffield Centre for all your help and support; likewise the Fresh Expressions team.

Contents

Foreword

'Lucy does it again' sounds like a children's novel, but once again she has combined a sense of irrepressible fun and eye-catching creativity —and then mixed it with important and serious exploration of ways onward.

Many people admit that church, as they often know it, is not working well. Messy Church has come along as something that many groups could do and now have done. It's a significant start, but Lucy is rightly dissatisfied with that and recognizes the opportunity and weakness. Christendom has many faults, but one is being too easily satisfied with church attendance as a measure of being Christian. Just getting people to come to a Messy Church event can only be a beginning. One lesson of the earlier Family Service movement is that those who came monthly with their kids didn't usually progress to weekly 'normal Sunday' and, when their kids grew out of it, they stopped too. It would be a tragedy to repeat that process. So this book is essential reading for any Messy Church fans. Another virtue is that it takes Messy Church seriously as a Fresh Expression of church in its own right. People need to grow within it and not just beyond it. So Lucy works with Messy Church's own characteristic values, alongside the generic ones that all churches need. She then rightly teases out how those values can be expressed in homes between monthly events, and how members of Messy Church live out a whole-life following of Jesus that will affect the world around them for good.

The book will help a wide range of people because it contains the reflective and practical. It has balance—and realism about what is sustainable by volunteers with the need to think long-term thoughts toward maturity. It goes beyond 'attractional' church to a discipleship that will be key for all expressions of church.

George Lings, Director of Church Army's research unit—the Sheffield Centre

6

Introduction

It's rather fun to be writing this second *Messy Church* book. When I wrote the first one, Messy Church was something very small and precious, personal and precarious, and we had no idea what would happen. But what an exciting journey it's been over the last few years: meeting many of you through Barnabas training days, at Messy Fiesta events, and online via email and www.messychurch.org.uk. With this book I feel as if I'm writing to a group of friends. And right at the outset I want to say a huge 'thank you' to you all for your generosity, warmth, willingness to share and graciousness in bearing with us the many times we go wrong or set off down a wrong track. I'm quite sure we'll be making mistakes all the time we're running Messy Churches, and it's kind of you to stick with us as we work out together how best to build this project up and help more and more people to enjoy loving Jesus together.

Throughout the book, I've tried to avoid using the word 'family' because of the misconceptions that the word can sometimes evoke. Too often, it can be understood exclusively as the nuclear unit of mum, dad and children, even if we all know that family can mean all sorts of combinations of people who depend on each other—grandparents and grandchildren, single-parent families, carers and children to mention only a few. But at the same time, one of the strengths and glories of the Messy Church identity is that it is a church for the whole family, household or whatever you want to call it, rather than being a place that encourages individualism, separatism and homogeneity. It is a place where all ages are valued and where everyone gains from being in contact with people of other ages. In this book, I've replaced 'family' with 'people', although the word doesn't have quite the same significance. So please read every mention of 'people' as a weighted term that understands 'family' in its broadest and best sense.

First of all (and just in case your copy of *Messy Church* was whisked away by keen crafty people before you had time to read it), let's recap on the Messy Church model outlined in the first book. Messy Church in its original form is a Fresh Expression of church that began in an Anglican church in Portsmouth as a way of being church for people who don't do traditional church, for whatever reason. It is church for all ages: adults are welcome with a child in tow, or vice versa. It meets after school once a month on a Thursday and goes as follows:

3.30–4.00	arrivals, drinks, board games, chat
4.00–5.00	crafts
5.00–5.15	celebration in church
5.15–5.45	hot meal

Since Messy Church began in 2004, the *Fresh Expressions* DVD and the previous book have meant that lots of churches have picked up on the idea and been able to adapt it for their own situation, both in the UK and overseas (at the time of writing, Canada, New Zealand and Australia), which we still find ridiculously exciting.

Of course, where it's been springing up in other parishes and different contexts, it happens on different days of the week and sometimes with different names. In Christchurch, New Zealand, they call it Families@4, for example. And from Gisburn, the Reverend Eric Kyte wrote, 'One lesson they learnt thanks to my father-in-law was to change the title. He saw "Messy Church 4–6pm" and said, "Church? Two hours? I can't think you'll get many takers!' He was right: we changed the name to Whatever Club, while still being upfront about what it was, and, lo and behold, a good crowd turned out!'

WHY A SECOND BOOK?

So what's the purpose of a second book? Partly to provide another set of themed sessions (you've probably read that part of the book first!) to save planning groups time and to make the best use of existing ideas. Many thanks to the creative imagination of our planning team for the ideas here. But the purpose of this book is mostly to encourage us all to be dissatisfied and to want more for the adults and children we're working with. It's fantastic that your Messy Church is welcoming people who wouldn't otherwise light up the doors of a church, and you are doing a great job of affirming their identity as loved children of God, of creatively exploring God's word together, of helping them feel comfortable with putting worship into words and of deepening fellowship by eating together. Good! Brilliant! In fact—essential! But as we all go on with Messy Church, it becomes increasingly clear that we need to carry on gently opening up appropriate ways for people to go further and deeper with God. In other words, how can we help them grow as disciples?

To do this, we need to look to the wisdom and resources of the Church through history but we also need to look imaginatively at the particular context we are in today and to have the vision and courage to develop new forms of discipleship that are suited to the context of the people who come to Messy Church. So in this book, we'll be looking at the 'what next?' question, starting the debate on what might be appropriate forms of discipleship for adults and children to walk in together, and how we might enable them to do so through the relationships and structures that we've built up in Messy Church.

The growth of Messy Churches means that there's a corresponding need to meet and share ideas with other leaders and helpers so that we can continue to let the concept grow and develop. One way we've done this through Barnabas is by setting up www.messychurch.org.uk, which is a sharing place for crafts, recipes, ideas and problems. Another way is by holding Messy Fiestas across the country. These are days of sharing, learning from each other and celebrating all that God is doing. And, of course, there's this, the second book, which ponders on the question 'What next?' It's a very exciting time to be in the Church, with the Spirit of God blasting fresh air in from all directions, and things are changing even as I write this introduction, never mind by the time the book's in your hands.

SO... WHAT NEXT?

One of the things we're all learning in Fresh Expressions is the need to go one step at a time. God's kingdom wasn't built in a day and if you don't build on a solid foundation the whole thing—even with the best intentions in the world—will wobble, waste time and money and be generally dispiriting. So when you are starting out with Messy Church, it's absolutely right to begin by throwing everything you have into making the once-a-month meeting time the most engaging it can be, without worrying about 'What next?' Three times so far on our own 'messy' journey, God has spoken to me (twice through other people and once through Psalm 23 at a friend's induction service, of all places) to say, basically, 'Don't *worry*. Just keep on doing what you're doing. You're doing a great job.' And I believe now that those words are for all of us. You'll know when it's time to develop things further.

The Fresh Expressions team has described a typical process that many new churches find they are replicating. You can see it in brighter colours on the Fresh Expressions website. It goes like this. When people are searching for a way to start reaching out to those in a particular context, the pattern is often:

Listening and following God's call ➤ loving service ➤ forming community ➤ disciple-making ➤ evolving worship

All this is surrounded by prayer and support, and 'connection' underpins the whole process.

I would suggest that people who are setting up Messy Churches and running them as described in the first book are doing a grand job in the first three stages: Listening and following God's call—loving service—forming community. You are doing fantastic outreach and it is a crucial first step in itself: we need to build up trust and relationships before we can go further. But some way down the line, do we stay content with the once-a-month contact? What we want to do, when the time is right and God is prodding, is to provide the opportunity for people to go deeper with God and to show them that there is a path of discipleship within or beyond Messy Church that they may want to explore with us.

Things move very slowly for us, as those of you who read the blog on the Messy Church website will know. I blame it on our lack of a paid administrator or family worker, but I suspect, in the dark reaches of the night, that it is my lack of organization. It might also be that we are a little bit like the goose at the front of the migrating V, or the person picking their way through the swamp to show the others a path: perhaps all pioneers feel the same way. It might take lots of wrong turns to arrive at what looks, in hindsight, like the obvious way forward. We're also operating in real life, not some idealized ecclesiastical dream world, and have to fit Messy Church in with being the taxi service for teenagers, holding down jobs and tending to senior members of the family—as, indeed, I'm sure you do too. All very Paul the tentmaker-esque.

But the long and the short of it is, we haven't got a 'Eureka! Sorted!' solution to the question of discipleship that we've tried and tested. As I write, we are setting out on a tentative foray into discipleship, but it could go pear-shaped. We do spend a lot of time reflecting on the opportunities and bounce the reflections off wise people. And it's these reflections that we want to share now, in the hope that, as you go forward with your Messy Churches, you'll be encouraged to go deeper in discipleship and to share your different ideas with everyone else.

CHAPTER 1

Messy discipleship: possible ways forward

What I'd like to do is suggest a possible framework for the way forward. I'm not going to recommend a 'one size fits all' solution to encouraging discipleship, because we all need to get excited about what is right for our own situation. (While I'm delighted that so many churches have found the Messy Church model useful, I am a little disappointed not to hear of any nascent gardening/sports/chocolate churches, which would mean that people had really personalized and localized the concept. However, not only is there plenty of evidence that people are adapting the Messy Church model to suit their own situations, but other Fresh Expressions of church are popping up all over, which is a cause of much rejoicing.

So I will suggest big-picture ideas to think about in your planning teams, keeping the very specific Messy Church situation firmly in mind, and I hope that between us, with the networks of Messy Fiestas, the website and local friendships between Messy Churches, we will come up with many imaginative and creative ways of helping to transform people's lives over the coming years. I hope as well, perhaps arrogantly, that as our church in England—Methodist, URC, Anglican and other denominations—explores how to be church for our changing culture, looking back to valuable traditions and forward to making a church for very different societies, our joint discoveries through Messy Church might perhaps help other churches work out how best to help adults and children to walk with Jesus together in the future.

THE BIG PICTURE

Let's take a look at the big picture of what we're doing long-term in Messy Church. For example:

✢ What are we aiming for?
✢ How will we recognize 'success' when it happens?
✢ How might we go about making disciples?
✢ What about the team itself?

What are we aiming for?

As we look across the babbling hubbub of colour and action in our Messy Church, do we ever think about what we would like to be seeing in five years' time? Are we dreaming dreams? Do we dream of adults and children plodding in through the doors and through the 'messy' process like sardines in a canning factory? Is that as good as it gets? Oh dear! Have we become fishers of people for our own dastardly sardines-on-toast purposes? (Or to make our church look good/be seen to care for those on the fringe/increase numbers and so on?) I don't think so.

Wouldn't we love instead to see families—adults and children, and individuals—changed, transformed and healed, with doors opened to them that they'd never imagined? Life in all its fullness, as bright as the rainbow of paints in a paintbox, in front of them, and a vivid and articulated friendship with Jesus shining out of them. People who have gained the confidence to take hold of the paintbrush and make a mark. People who are like playdough in the skilled sculptor's hands and recognize his gentle creativity everywhere they go. People with a sense of contentedness and satisfaction from being fed on food that lasts, and yet who are hungry for more. People who want other people to taste and see and make and stick and praise and live because it's so good. People who are in it for the long haul, even when the going gets tough. People with a growing and active compassion for others in

13

playgrounds, workplaces, homes and nations who don't yet have that sense of safety, belonging and purpose. People whose love bubbles out of a Messy Church and into the rest of their lives. People who can change the world.

Reflect on your Messy Church
Imagine Jesus walking in among the people there. What parts of Messy Church would make him laugh? Who would he spend most time with? Who would he reach out to heal? Who would he confront? How would different people react to him?

How will we recognize 'success' when it happens?

Alarm bells clang at the word 'success' in this context. It feels so Pharisaic and seems just on the brink of the numbers game that we so often play in churches: 'It's big so it must be good! ... Numbers are low: it's obviously not working.' Many Messy Churches have huge numbers of people through the doors from the word go. Indeed, in Morden, the first session they ran brought in 120 people and the 'full up' sign had to go outside! (I wouldn't have liked to be on the cooks' team that day.) But it's very dangerous to claim that this is a mark of success in itself. Having all those people is a great opportunity, certainly, and a successful first step, but the way God's kingdom measures success is more about maturity than numbers. And we are in this for the long haul, not for a short sharp shock, so success is better seen as making the most of each step of the journey, rather than ever feeling that we have arrived.

Maturity, then, not numbers, is an aim in the long term. A shorthand definition of maturity within Christianity might be that the more mature you are, the more you love. But that would be too easy to trot out tritely and sentimentally. Here's what George Lings writes about maturity of whole churches in an essay on 'Fresh Expressions growing to maturity':

Being church seems to be the result of what happens when people encounter Jesus in such a way that it transforms them to become more like him and so also transforms their relationships with one another. In one sense maturity is the process of growing up into Christ, becoming in practice what by change of status we already are. It is a long, undulating process with spiritual, moral and social dimensions. Maturity is connected to integrity and authenticity, for mature behaviour and reactions have a health, balance and cohesion that are attractive. It is also linked to awareness of self-identity and self-knowledge. So churches that demonstrate maturity will also have a good idea of what church is, what it is for and what it is like when healthy.

We do want our Messy Churches to mature and to develop in every dimension, in the way also described in the same essay:

✣ A dimension called UP: seeking God, to become more like him in his holiness.
✣ A dimension called IN: growing a community that reflects the diverse oneness of the Trinity.
✣ A dimension called OUT: that embodies the apostolic community living out being sent.
✣ A dimension called OF: knowing each expression belongs as part of the catholic wider whole.[1]

For this to be real from the grass roots up, we want the people who belong to Messy Church to become individually mature. Here's George Lings again: 'Following Christ is the walk, growing like Christ is the aim.'[2]

For our very varied congregations, some of the following way markers might be useful guides as we try to spot people walking forward in their discipleship. These are not rules or regulations, just the sort of things that might indicate God's working—like leaf buds on a tree in springtime.

How are people reacting to Jesus?

Are people changing in the way they react when you talk about Jesus? Are they starting to talk about him themselves? Are you seeing a difference in the way people engage with worship/story/prayer during the whole Messy Church session? Can you sense a deeper engagement, a curiosity, a looking forward to this aspect of what you do? For example, are people offering to lead part of the event or offering to be more deeply involved? Are people enthused to puzzle over the Bible and question it? Has anyone shown an interest in studying the Bible?

How are people reacting to other people?

Are you seeing a deepening concern for and understanding of what it means to be a neighbour; a growing concern for local issues and global ones? Are there times when you've spotted peacemakers at work? Is there a growing respect for other people, a concern for personal relationships, friendships, family relationships; a willingness to build up, not break down? Is there an increased understanding of and trust in God's healing power?

How are people changing in their creativity?

Do you sense more willingness to 'have a go' at the different creative activities you have on offer? Is there more readiness to risk or to play?

How are people changing in their attitude to the created world?

Are they seeing more of its beauty? Are they more concerned for its well-being? Do they relate what they believe to the way they live their life on a fragile planet?

Reflect on your Messy Church
What examples of any of the above have you spotted? Talk as a team. Write them down before you forget. If they're not confidential, do send them to the website community to encourage others (www.messychurch.org.uk).

How might we go about making disciples?

For his dissertation *Making Disciples in Fresh Expressions*, Andrew Roberts listened to twelve leaders of different sorts of Fresh Expressions to find out what they do to make disciples in their different settings. He found that leaders believe their congregations need three main things to become disciples or to walk further on their discipleship journey. These three things need to be culturally relevant to help form mature whole-life disciples. They are:

✢ A sacramental environment
✢ Supportive relationships
✢ Intentional learning

In other words, we need to provide a safe, holy space where God is both there and 'other', present and transcendent; a community where people build each other up; and a way of learning together about things of faith.

The examples he uses are from churches that don't specialize in making an effort to include all ages, but the principles are equally fine ones to work from for Messy Church. We just need to think about how they work in an all-age way. All three elements are potentially part of Messy Church to some extent, and it's good to reinforce the usefulness of what we're doing when we meet together.

For example, we provide a safe space, where there is encouragement to take risks and be creative, where we can worship in different ways and meet God in other people, in his word and in his gracious provision of food. (We will look at the importance of food at greater length later on, and think about the whole question of sacraments.) We provide the opportunity for supportive, all-age, cross-generational relationships to flourish, encouraging older people to enjoy being with and learning from younger ones, and vice versa. We base our programmes on Bible stories and approach them with an attitude of learning in different ways, suitable for the culture we're dealing with.

It's a good start. However, we all know that there is always room for improvement, and we come up against the fact that we only meet once a month, so what can be done to encourage discipleship in the other 30 or so days of the month?

Reflect on your Messy Church
Who are disciples among the people who come to Messy Church? How do you know? Who's still sitting in the waiting room, train-spotting? Who hasn't even noticed there's a journey to go on?

What next?

So we have the start of something whole-life, which does a crucial and valuable job but doesn't yet go the whole way. We have set ourselves limits by holding Messy Church just once a month—and this is very deliberate! It's good to know your limits, and our team can only just cope with one a month; we couldn't offer Messy Church every week. A vicar from another church was talking recently about her congregation's plans to start up a Messy Church. She said, 'But our parents work, it would have to be at a weekend, and have we got enough leaders to run it every Sunday afternoon?' I said, 'Um, it would only be once a month, though, wouldn't it?' and suddenly the thing became doable for them. However, what about the rest of the month? How are we helping our Messy Church people to feel they belong to a church family in those days? How are we encouraging them to walk the discipleship walk when they're not actually at Messy Church?

Notes

1 George Lings, 'Fresh Expressions growing to maturity', in Steven Croft (ed.), *The Future of the Parish System: Shaping the Church of England in the 21st Century* (Church House Publishing, 2006), p. 138.
2 George Lings, 'Unravelling the DNA of church: How can we know that what is emerging is "church"?' in *International Journal for the Study of the Christian Church*, Vol. 6, No.1, March 2006.

CHAPTER 2

Discipleship in the home

Discipleship in the home is not a well-explored area in the UK. There is plenty on discipling children and even more on discipling adults. (The sense of inflicting discipleship on someone, implied by the verb, reminds me of a glorious moment at a training day, where a very loud lady demanded to know where the 'Disciplining children' workshop was being held. 'Er, there isn't one,' said the host. 'Do you mean "Discipling children"?' 'But that's not what I want at all,' came the reply. 'I want to know how to sort them out when they're naughty.')

At the Messy Fiestas, it has been interesting to ask whether people have been brought up in a Christian home and, if they have, how do they know? 'My parents took me to church' is the standard answer. Only a very few people reply that their mother or father would pray with them or that they read the Bible together, even that they would say grace at meal times. No one I have spoken to said that they talked about God at home. All overtly Christian activity seems to have happened within the confines of a church building rather than in the home. Of course, it would be unfair to deny the value of the unspoken 'givens' of a family life, the values that are so deeply rooted that they remain unarticulated although they are implied in everything the household does. But is this very English, very unexpressed assumption of belief necessarily the best thing for growing disciples in the next generation?

In the United States, there has been more research on ways to build up discipleship in the home, but for the British culture there

20

are very few well-trodden paths to follow. At the time of writing, only a handful of books on this subject from the UK are readily available. The Church has traditionally taken over the role of parents and carers in bringing up children to follow Jesus, and has elbowed the carers out into a position of powerlessness. Christian education is done in church, isn't it? At Sunday school? We're not qualified to do it at home: we'll leave it to the experts... So many of us are left not knowing how to go about bringing up our children in a Christian home, because no one ever read the Bible to us when we were little, or prayed with us, or felt that anything more than taking us to church and getting us confirmed was required.

Wouldn't it be fantastic, through our Messy Church networks, to rebuild a discipleship in our country that works from the home out, that comes from the heart of a home-based ministry? A discipleship that lasts for generations as our children teach their children, that shows parents and grandparents how to be the family of God right at the heart of home life. An environment where adults and children expect to learn about Jesus from each other, to be encouraged by each other to stick with him and to bring joys and sorrows to him together. This would be a rooted, genuine experience of God that would enrich corporate church life and strengthen it from within, to outlast any temporary glitches in its effectiveness. Put bluntly, if the Church were to crumble, would faith go on? Maybe that is what Messy Church is here for in the long term.

A really brilliant English book on this subject is *The Heavenly Party* by Michele Guinness (Monarch, 2007). I wish I could reproduce the whole lot here, because it's superb and wise and wonderful and will inspire you to great things. Michele shows how the Jewish people have always celebrated festivals in the home and as a community, rather than getting all institutionalized, and she demonstrates with loads of imaginative but doable ideas how we as Christians can celebrate our festivals, too, both in the home and in the community. In fact, you come away from the book feeling that every night is party night—no bad thing at all. There are also some luscious recipes to use at home or at Messy Church: bring 'em on!

MESSY CHURCH VALUES

As we think about the whole question of discipleship, of encouraging and enabling our 'messy' congregations to grow in maturity, what practical approaches could we take? The once-a-month Messy Church is going fine. You will be inspired, no doubt, to make changes and develop successes as you go along, but essentially it will probably be OK not to fiddle with the main structure for a while. We decided that we wanted to encourage prayer and storytelling during the Thursday Messy Church, without getting authoritative about it. Our (not brilliant) solution was to add nothing except a quiet corner: a beach tent and rug with some comfy cushions, a prayer book to write in and some good-quality children's Bible storybooks to read. Our problem is that our room isn't terribly well adapted for making quiet corners and nooks that are safe, accessible and open as well as being something of a sanctuary (it would probably be much easier to set aside a quiet space in a cranny-riddled ancient church). But we're flagging up something subliminally—that we think space and quiet is as important as mess and noise.

Another church, in Brixham in Devon, cleverly uses its church building to include just such a spot, where a quiet candle-making activity always happens and where candles are lit and prayers said before people move on to their next activity. This has grown out of one person's quiet inspiration and personal spirituality. And another church, in Dronfield in Derbyshire, regularly sets up a small lounge room as a quiet space, with a gentle prayer activity such as floating candles in a paddling pool, where people can have time out from the busyness and noise of the messier crafts.

You will think of ways to build more opportunities for meeting God into the structure you have. But we want to use the other 30 days of the month, without swamping busy people with more meetings. George Lings suggested that to develop the Messy Church ethos into the rest of the month we should build on the *values* behind what we do. He rather tongue-in-cheekily suggested that our values as a church are that we:

✢ Chill
✢ Create
✢ Celebrate
✢ Chew (or chomp)

I'm sure, in other forms of church, leaders find loftier and nobler-sounding values than chilling and chomping. However, in the once-a-month Messy Church model, although the values all occur to a greater or lesser extent in the other areas, too, these values are found primarily in the following shapes.

✢ **Chilling** is in the welcome time together, where everyone is welcomed and encouraged just to chat.
✢ **Creating** is in the crafts.
✢ **Celebrating** is in the simple act of worship.
✢ **Chewing** is in the sharing of food.

As these values have proved wholesome and helpful in our outreach to others, can we find ways of encouraging those values in other shapes as discipleship in the rest of the month? Every context is different and every church has different resources and expectations. But, between us, surely we can discover some good ways of helping adults and children to follow Jesus together in the home.

Here are some ideas.

Messy monks

Well, not quite! But certainly in other forms of Fresh Expressions, a monastic-style 'rule of life' is catching on as a way of encouraging people to live Christ day-to-day. Not a Fresh Expression, but one example that has been tried and tested, is the Franciscan Third Order. (Do a web search on it and find out their approach.) A rule of life is normally a very personal, individual approach within the context of a wider community, but our situation is that we want to suggest ways in which adults and children can follow Christ *together* within a wider community. With a little imagination and creativity, the principle can be a very positive one, encouraging people to belong to Christ and to Messy Church more than just once a month.

Here's a pattern for introducing this idea.

1. Your planning group meets and discusses the four values of Messy Church (chill, create, celebrate, chew) and understands how they form the shape of what you do in Messy Church once a month.
2. You discuss whether the time has come to introduce an element of discipleship in the home to your own Messy Church.
3. You look at the lists of possible activities (see pages 26–27) to encourage following Jesus in the home through the four values, and add better ones that are more relevant and localized for your area and 'messy' congregation. (For example, you might suggest a walk in a specific park or going to see a particular film that's on this month.)
4. You make a copy of one suggestion from each list for each person on an attractive card.
5. At Messy Church, include the Messy Church 'faith in the home' sign-up (see opposite) as one of the activities. Everyone who signs up is given their card showing the month's challenges or ideas. Encourage them to give the ideas a try and report back next month on how they got on.
6. During the following months, build in time for a designated person to talk with people during Messy Church about how they got on and how they've got to know Jesus better. Depending on your circumstances, you might do this very informally or you might set up a 'telling table', with a wise mentor to hand, and ask participants to go and talk to the mentor, who will then give them the card showing the next month's challenges or ideas. The mentor might like to say a short unthreatening prayer with each person somewhere in the process.

Here's an example of a 'Faith in the home' sign-up card.

Messy Church

Faith in the home

We

....

....

would like to follow Jesus more closely together.

We meet Jesus when we:

Chill together
So we will enjoy spending time together and with other Christians

Create together
So we will enjoy making things and exploring God's wonderful world

Celebrate together
So we will find ways of enjoying God's word in the Bible and talking to him

Chew together
So we will enjoy eating together and with others

Witnessed

....

Date ....

Here are the lists of possible activities to get you going.

Chilling or chewing

Ideas that will help people to enjoy being together in the home.

✣ We'll stay in one night and watch a DVD together (with popcorn).
✣ We'll each invite a friend and have a takeaway.
✣ We'll borrow a cookery book and try out a new recipe.
✣ We'll invite someone who is lonely round for a meal.
✣ We'll light a candle when we eat together, to remember Jesus.
✣ We'll go without something we all enjoy for one week and make a donation to a local charity for those who are homeless.
✣ We'll do something none of us has done before.
✣ We'll have five minutes of just being quiet with each other and with God.
✣ We'll say hello to someone in our street we don't yet know.
✣ We'll go cloud-watching or stargazing together.
✣ We'll buy something fairly traded that we haven't yet tried.
✣ We'll put a penny in a jar for every good thing we have in a week and give the money away.

Creating

Ideas to encourage people to make something or enjoy something created.

✣ We'll try to make something together every Sunday this month.
✣ One week this month, we will make a prayer sculpture out of pipe cleaners, which we add to each day.
✣ We'll make a cake together to bring to Messy Church next month.
✣ We'll listen to some music together.
✣ We'll go to the cinema or theatre or for a walk together.
✣ We'll go on to the website of a charity we like and see if they have any suggestions for things to make.

✣ We'll make something that will help the world we live in, such as a mini-beast house or a bird table.
✣ We'll start a family scrapbook for all the things we want to treasure and remember.
✣ We'll take a photo or draw a picture of the people and pets who live in our home.
✣ We'll write our names inside a cross-shape and put it up on the kitchen wall.

Celebrating

Ideas to help people live close to God and live life in all its fullness.

✣ We'll say grace before meals for one whole week.
✣ We'll throw a party.
✣ We'll read a Bible story each day for a week and talk about it together.
✣ We'll set up a prayer corner in the house.
✣ We'll collect some natural things from the park or garden or wood, and make something beautiful out of them.
✣ We'll send a card to someone we value.
✣ We'll talk about what gifts God has given each one of us.
✣ We'll give some money away.
✣ We'll watch the news together and thank God for anything that is a sign of his kingdom.
✣ We'll make up a song about what we like about Jesus.
✣ We'll invite someone along to the next Messy Church.

Identity

Perhaps we need to keep reminding people that they belong to Messy Church during the rest of the month by way of non-verbal messages in the home. This was one of the reasons why we decided, after a lot of thought, to provide some 'branded' merchandise. They are tangible things that go out of church and back into homes to act as memory joggers, just as having a mug with Pompey or Manchester United on it reminds you which team you support and says something about belonging to a permanent wider 'family'.

Of course, the individual craft items made at Messy Church go back into homes, and we regularly make something that encourages some sort of spiritual action, so any ready-made merchandise is icing on the cake. We began with a few tentative suggestions for merchandise that might come in handy either at Messy Church or to send back into homes as presents. We're small enough to be flexible and respond to what you think would be useful, so keep sending your ideas in! Could you strategically use a Messy Church pencil, badge, mug or car sticker to help reinforce a sense of belonging?

Learning

One aspect of being church where we arguably fall short is in our 'head learning' together—the sort of learning that involves thinking and brainwork, not learning experientially or emotionally (both of which are equally important alongside the brainy stuff). What we do in Messy Church is a great start, as we explore together the key stories of Jesus, key doctrines of the Church and images of God through crafts and story, but we need to make sure that we encourage people to keep moving on and growing, learning in every way God has given us. I don't think anyone would argue that a quarter of an hour's study per month in any subject, from learning to read to nuclear physics, is going to be enough. So how do we encourage people to keep learning about God together?

There are plenty of routes to try out. You might choose one of the following suggestions, but you may also have others of your own.

Rent-a-mentor

Each person who wants to join in is provided with a mentor (obviously at no charge: 'rent-a' is purely a nice rhyme with 'mentor') —a mature Christian, or family of Christians, to walk alongside them and encourage them. This might be a way for members of the Sunday congregation to play a part in supporting newer Christians. How they support them is best left to individuals to decide and discern, but might involve mutual hospitality, meeting together to share concerns and joys for prayer, and opening up the Bible together.

1. Your planning group makes a list of people from the church who might be safe and suitable mentors for Messy Church people.
2. You talk with these possible mentors and find out if they would be willing to be involved. If they are, you will need to apply for CRB clearance as soon as possible.
3. Gather your rent-a-mentors together and do any training necessary, including best practice for child protection and the fact that their main role is to be as encouraging and supportive to their protégés as possible: they are to be Christ to them in a way that the protégés feel comfortable with. You can give out a list of suggestions (see below), but these are only suggestions and your mentors may have better ideas.
4. Once you have some mentors ready to roll, explain at Messy Church what you'd like to offer. It is a good idea to start with something very easy and simple, like 'We'd like to start a rent-a-mentor scheme! There are people in our church who would love to get to know you, and be like an extra support to you all. If you'd like to rent-a-mentor, let me know.'
5. Once relationships have been established, encourage your rent-a-mentors to talk sensitively about Jesus, open up the Bible, tell stories about him, and bring Jesus into the conversations they have with their protégés. Make sure they know that this may well be the only time in the week that their protégés get to learn about God.

Ideas for mentors include:

✤ Learn the names and ages of your protégés.
✤ Pray for them each day.
✤ Find out what they would like prayer for.
✤ Pop round or ring up once a month to find out how they are: you might take a little treat like a small box of chocolates or biscuits, or just an invitation to the next Messy Church or other event.
✤ Invite them for a cup of tea or juice with good-quality cake.
✤ Get your church to find some suitable Bible reading notes or children's books about Jesus and take a copy to your protégés.
✤ Take round a CD of children's worship songs from the church library.
✤ Respond to clues: you might have a skill children would like to learn, like knitting, or time on your hands to babysit for an hour while their mum goes to the shops, or a car that you could use to take their mum to the shops. Listen for worries and anxieties.
✤ If appropriate, ask for a photo of your protégés.
✤ Share your pet, or offer to pet-sit.
✤ Most of all, listen.

Messy munch

Being part of a small group seems to be one of the most effective ways that people are growing as Christian disciples in similar contexts to Messy Church. Two or three people choose to meet during the month to explore the Bible together in a way that they can all engage with. People with younger children might get together over coffee and juice and explore stories and issues using reflective storytelling, art and craft for active group members, while more sedentary ones discuss questions in a more abstract way. People with older children might have a time of marshmallows, crisps, beer and Coke and a Bible-based discussion that engages everyone and values all contributions from young and old.

1. Make a list of people already on the Christian journey and another of people who are just setting out or just thinking about it. Are there any obvious pairings or groupings? Friendships are always a good starting point, and a similar age of children helps, too.
2. Talk to people who have already set out on the Christian journey and enthuse them about giving 'messy munch' a try for, say, six months as an experiment. Work with them to sort out a programme suitable for their age bracket and social setting for these six months: it might simply be to talk about the story you explored at Messy Church last time and to read it for themselves, discussing it in a way that suits their group. Swap the leadership round between ages and sexes each time. Begin with a short prayer and end with suggestions for prayer from everyone in the group. Open-ended questions, such as the suggestions below, are great with all but the very youngest children.

   - What do you find most interesting about this story?
   - What do you find most puzzling?
   - What do you think is most important in this story?
   - What do you think God is saying to you through it?

3. Introduce the idea of 'messy munch' from the front at Messy Church, saying what you are offering and why you are offering it. People themselves invite the specific 'setting out' fellow members to join them for a six-month trial.
4. If appropriate, you might want to offer some Messy Church funds towards the food and drink for the 'messy munches'. The children or teens could be in charge of spending it wisely.

Dotcom discipleship

One of the glories of modern technology is the opportunity to 'meet' online, meaning that people do not have to worry about babysitting but can carry on a meeting in the comfort of their own home. Following an online discipleship course together, meeting online regularly and face-to-face occasionally, might not only interest some of the men who can't make Messy Church, but could also make it possible for people to take their own responsibility for learning, still within the supportive framework of a group. While there isn't yet an all-age course, something like Foundations21 has such a rich variety of material and activities that there is plenty for all ages to enjoy (see www.foundations21.org.uk) .

1. Find out whether there is any funding available from your church, deanery, circuit or area for Christian education and outreach, and apply for it.
2. Make a list of people you think would benefit from following the course (for a set length of time, to start with). Decide (if it's a paying course) how you want to cover costs. Decide who from the core team could serve as a mentor or convener.
3. Decide how you might meet once a month with participating people face-to-face to discuss how they are all getting on (perhaps over a meal, cheese and wine / lemonade, or coffee and cake).
4. At Messy Church, introduce the idea of exploring following Jesus together and use a computer to show what course or website you have in mind. Make clear what the commitment is and ask people personally as well as generally.
5. Plan to start soon enough to catch the enthusiasm, but far enough off to give people time to get their heads around the idea, or consult with spouses, teens who don't come to Messy Church and so on, to get them all on board.

Run a course

Adapt a ready-made 'professional' course to make it engaging for all ages, running it alongside Messy Church at a similar time but on another week. I leave this to your imagination and conscience, as certain organizations get twitchy if you alter their prepared package. Perhaps, over the next few years, there will be some suitable courses designed for all-age learning.

You may sense that I am not over-keen on the 'get people on a course' approach, perhaps because we've never had any success in getting people from Messy Church on to an Alpha or Emmaus course. Perhaps it feels out of kilter with the whole 'messy' approach of letting discipleship happen gradually and in relationship, rather than through the comparative hot-housing of a course. The courses are fantastic resources and just right for people in other situations, but I'm not sure how appropriate they are for our all-age approach.

Messy takeaway menus

This is perhaps the simplest idea to put into operation. I've supplied some suggestions in this book for taking the theme of the session back into homes, under the 'takeaway menu' at the end of each unit, but you will have lots of your own to add. You might choose simply to copy them out on cards for people to take home and leave it at that; you might programme them into one of the suggestions above (a course or a mentoring scheme). You might combine this with the 'messy monks' idea on page 23. You might also provide a take-home bag with things that would make it easier to do—for example, the raw materials of a craft, a tealight candle, some website addresses, or a CD, book or DVD to borrow and bring back next time. Many schools send young children home with a story sack, so many people will understand the general principle.

CONCLUDING THOUGHTS

Obviously, it's completely up to you whether you decide to use any of these ideas or not, and how you decide to use them.

You might (justifiably) throw up your hands in horror and say, 'We're up to our ears with sorting out Messy Church once a month. Enough is enough!' And if that is how you feel, you are most probably right. Yes, really. Don't stress about it, just simply enjoy what you're doing already. If, or when, it's time to do something different, God will nudge you in the right direction at the right time and give you the energy and the people to do it. What matters is being childlike, enjoying being fully in the present, not fretting about what you did wrong in the past or how you're going to cope with the future.

Discipleship is messy. It's hard to see that you'll have anyone who neatly walks the narrow path and jumps docilely through every hoop you provide. You may not even be able to notice the way God is leading someone into a transformed lifestyle and drawing them closer to him. You are doing a very difficult job, one which, as far as we can tell, has been practised very little in the UK, where discipleship in the home is a relatively unknown phenomenon. It is easier to 'do discipleship' to someone else than to walk beside them on the road or call to them from the top of a hill. It is easier to control people and shove them through a course or process than to listen to them, pray with them and grow with them, especially if they're a quarter of your age. It's easier to build on the sand than on the rock. It would be much easier to hold tightly to the reins and just do Messy Church once a month for ever and ever. However, the Holy Spirit is not only comforting but restless, and will probably be inspiring you to take things further when the time is right.

✢ Build from a firm foundation: get your relationships and your community on a firm footing before you start building on it.
✢ Work into homes rather than imposing more external gatherings.
✢ Expect the unexpected, because God works like that, especially with the least likely people.
✢ Work for your children's grandchildren: we're in this, whatever form it changes into, for the long haul.
✢ Keep being transformed by the renewing of your imagination and stay flexible and open to God's whisper for the changes he needs you to make, and to recognize the changes in others.

CHAPTER 3

Messy teams

What about the team itself? How do you keep the enthusiasm up after the excitement has worn off (which might be after one month or after three years)? How do you ensure that your team is as well equipped as possible for the important ministry they have to do? How do you thank them? How do you include them all in the ownership of Messy Church without killing yourself trying to consult everyone on every decision?

Set out below are some suggestions of what you can do, and what Barnabas can do as an organization to help you.

PRAYER

I am completely useless at formal organized praying and encouraging the team to pray, but that doesn't stop me knowing that prayer is crucial for all aspects of Messy Church. Whether or not God provides neat answers to the sort of prayers that go, 'Lord, we really need Asda to have unflavoured popcorn and googly eyes for this Thursday', praying does keep things in perspective on the bigger front. It's rather like those diagrams of unmagnetized needles that we used to draw in Physics, with all the particles facing any old way in a confused manner, until you stroke them with a magnet and they shuffle round gradually to face north–south in a useful and organized way. Prayer gets us facing the right way, reminds us what our purpose is and makes us useful by a power outside our control. When there's a danger of getting fed up with the 'mechanics' of Messy Church, it's worth checking out how much prayer has been put in recently, both individually and as a team. In the spirit of the four values of Messy Church, how about holding a chilling, creating, celebrating, chewing prayer meeting?

Messy prayer meeting

1. Welcome people in with tasty drinks and savoury snacks, suitable for different tastes and age groups (for some, Diet Coke and cheesy footballs are anathema; for others they are a mega-treat).
2. Talk about the highs and lows of recent Messy Church sessions.
3. Tell a short Bible story from a modern retelling.
4. Use a creative medium, such as playdough, pipe cleaners, tin foil, felt tips and so on. Ask people to think and talk to God privately while they make something out of that medium on the theme of one of the following:

   • Something they feel God is saying from the Bible story about Messy Church.
   • Something to express what they most want at Messy Church.
   • Something that is needed at Messy Church.
   • Something to give thanks to God for.
   • Something to say sorry for.

5. Have a tray or attractive cloth on a table and invite people to place their sculpture on the table as a way of giving that prayer to God, and, if they like, to say what it's about. If you have a memory like mine, write down what sort of things are coming out from the prayers.
6. Bring all the prayers together in a summing-up prayer, and finish with a celebratory snacky dessert, such as a chocolate fondue or fruit platter, a big fat cake or an ice cream. (I fear Messy Church will shortly be wholly responsible for the obesity of the nation. But it will be worth it. We wear it off in all the rushing around setting up chairs and tables, anyway.)

7. Keep a record of the concerns and outcomes of the prayers in a journal and check it every once in a while to be encouraged about what God has transformed without you even noticing.

A prayer that we gave out on bookmarks to our Sunday congregations runs as follows:

Dear God, you give us so much. Help Messy Church share your love with others. May each person feel the warmth of your welcome. May they share your joy of creation as they make things. May they love to hear your story and praise you. May they find your sustaining power in the nourishing food. Let each person grow in your love. And help all the leaders, young and old, to be Christ to them. Amen

(We don't ask for much, do we?)

ARE YOU LONESOME TONIGHT?

If you feel isolated, the once gleeful 'Whee! All these new people are meeting the Lord!' jollity and bonhomie can all too quickly become an attitude of 'Oh no, here come the ungrateful spongers again. Haven't they got homes to go to? Why bother with all this hard work? What's the point? I've run out of ideas. I've run out of oomph.' Your team might turn up faithfully to run a craft or to cook for 20 every month, but might lose sight of the reason for doing it all. Like the old analogy of a coal that's hopped out of the grate, it is hard to keep the fire flaming when you feel you are on your own. In a more edible analogy, the one remaining biscuit on the plate often feels a bit crumby.

Well, you are not on your own! You are a great team within your own church or group of churches, and there's a whole network of people out there waiting to welcome you with open arms.

In-house encouragement

Programme in a once-a-term evening for your whole team, from the cooks to the chair setter-uppers, from your grannies to your teenaged helpers, when you get together for a meal or nice nibbles and some feedback time. A simple framework of 'What's going well? What's going wrong?' will probably sort out most issues. It also makes sure that everyone feels they can have a say in what's going on, which gives ownership and increased commitment.

As and when specific training needs come up, you can respond to them. If you want to do it yourself, on the 'Barnabas in churches' website (www.barnabasinchurches.org.uk), under 'Articles', you'll find a whole library of useful training features which you might give out to your team to read and discuss. Barnabas produces a wide range of books to resource your children's work, as do other publishers. If you would rather call in an outsider, your diocesan children's adviser or equivalent may be able to provide input on the aspect of training you need. If not, you could contact us at Barnabas to see if one of the team is available to come to you (see page 224 for our contact details). There are also many other brilliant organizations that will provide inspirational training.

Wider encouragement

Barnabas provides events called Messy Fiestas. Here you can meet face-to-face with other Messy Church leaders, and people just setting out into Messy Church, who will share their ideas and problems and reassure you that you're not in this on your own. Messy Fiestas are a great opportunity to find out together what options there are for the way forward for 'messy' congregations, to learn some new crafts, pick up some new recipes and chew over some different options for dealing with the problems and opportunities we all face. Check out the website, www.messychurch.org.uk, for details of any Messy Fiesta events near you. If there aren't any planned, think about arranging one and inviting other Messy Churches from your area to come and join you.

The Messy Church website is also designed to encourage you and make it easier to find support from the wider network of Messy Churches. You can read all about other people's ideas and problems on the forum, keep up to date with any thinking on the blog, or check the website for other Messy Churches near you and go on a visit to refresh your vision and compare them with what you do. Whenever I've seen another Messy Church in action, I've always come away invigorated and inspired, usually because they have such good ideas that we can pinch, or *very* occasionally because I can gloat privately that we actually do something better than they do!

Thank you!

Small tokens of thanks are always appreciated: a card after a particularly hectic session, or a telephone call to say how much you appreciate someone's involvement, can encourage a team member mightily and help them feel appreciated. Your 'training meal' might also be part of the 'thank you' (I feel, subliminally, that a big fat pudding is a more graphic expression of thanks than a salad, though logically this is unreasonable.)

INVOLVEMENT

For the month-to-month planning, we find it works best to have a small planning group, like a sleek, well-oiled machine (stop laughing, team!) that knows what needs to get done and gets on with it. Other teams work differently. One Messy Church gets the whole team together for a once-a-year planning session for all the crafts at once, so that everyone can contribute and materials can be stocked up well in advance. It is wise to have some way in which team members can suggest ideas, even if it is just a Post-it note through the leader's door.

Younger leaders often work on a spur-of-the-moment basis and will come up with a storm of more or less brilliant ideas when they are actually doing Messy Church with you, whereas others need to sit and chew things over meditatively for hours before venturing a suggestion.

Organizationally, it helps to plan the planning meetings for the year as well as the dates of Messy Church. This not only means that your team can keep the planning dates free, but it will save you ringing round every time to tell everyone that a meeting is happening. If you also include the themes of the sessions on the timetable, people can be thinking ahead in terms of crafts and equipment and might be more inclined to come up with suggestions. This sounds so obvious, but took us three years to make happen. Alas.

Gifts

Messy Church gives churches the opportunity to let unexpected gifts come out of the cupboard. Who would have known that June has a spinning wheel or that Brian does some mean macramé? Who would have guessed that Robert would be so quietly fantastic in the kitchen? There is nothing like knowing that your gift is being used to the glory of God and for other people—it's a very energizing thing to happen to you. So it's worth making sure that you review the gifts of your team and wider congregation on a regular basis, particularly as you can expect your team to grow numerically and in maturity as they go about God's work month by month, and new gifts will be popping up all the time. There are many existing church resources for discovering your 'spiritual' gifts, but not so many for discovering your gifts if you believe that mountain-biking can be as spiritual as speaking in tongues.

Perhaps, as a fun and useful activity to do once in a while with your team, you could try the following suggestion. Personalize the list on page 42 and print it out. Add and take away from it to make it match your situation and people. These are some of the gifts we've found useful and usable in Messy Church, but you will want to add others or omit some things from the list. Leave plenty of space for names.

Give copies of the completed list to your team, one copy per two or three people. Say that God loves to see our gifts used in the service of other people and that it would be great to think about how we use the gifts he's given us, or how we could use those gifts at Messy Church. Give everyone 20 minutes to fill in the sheets (with their own names and other people's), then display them or pass them round. Each person can collect the results for one other member of the team and present them with their lists after looking at all the sheets. Then, together, with your own lists to look at, ask: are there any surprises… consistencies… inconsistencies?

After discussing the outcomes, give thanks to God for each person and the gifts he's given them, and pray together and on your own about whether you need to redeploy your team to different jobs.

GIFTS LIST

Gift	People who use it already	People who might well have it
Painting		
Drawing		
Sculpting		
Candle making		
Woodwork		
Sewing		
Modelling (making things)		
Big messy ideas		
Delicate ideas		
Coming up with ideas (imagination)		
Praying		
Dogs-bodying		
Brute strength		
A loud voice		
Partying		
Networking		
Singing		
Playing an instrument		
Dancing		
Acting		
Telling stories		
Getting on with people of all sorts		
Keeping things tidy		
Organizing		
Listening		
Chatting		
Cooking		

CHAPTER 4

FAQs

Here are some questions that have been frequently asked at some of the 'Introduction to Messy Church' sessions and at Messy Fiesta events.

HOW MUCH DOES IT COST?

This question usually refers to money, but, before we think about that, stand back a moment and consider other sorts of cost. Jesus was very down to earth about costs, telling parables about idiots who started building towers and couldn't afford to finish them, and kings working out how far they could go to war without bankrupting themselves. He also demanded everything from people who wanted to follow him and was brutally clear about what it would cost them: 'Do you really want to be homeless?' 'If you are serious about me, get rid of everything that is dear to you and walk away from what is familiar.' 'Can you die the death I'm going to die?'

One question that you will need to ask somewhere along the line (though not just as you start out) is how much you will invest in Messy Church. It may get to a point where, to develop and grow wider and deeper, it needs people who invest everything they have in it—people who commit to Messy Church as their main church, not just as an add-on to Sunday church. It needs people who leave their safe, familiar Sunday morning 10.30 nets on the shore and throw in their lot with this unpredictable venture. That will be the only way to really find out how far you can go with this shape of church.

At the moment, I'm not investing my whole spiritual welfare in

43

Messy Church: I've always got Sunday church to rely on for good worship, teaching, fellowship and so on. But what if I deliberately relied only on Messy Church? Wouldn't I be more determined to make something happen in it more than once a month? Yet the cost of leaving behind Sunday fellowship as my main area of belonging and resource would be massive. Just like the brave church planters who leave their sending church—just like Peter, James and John—it would be as big a step as that. That would be costly.

But to more mundane costs. At one Messy Church training day at another church, when I was waxing lyrical about the need to claim back everything spent on the session each time, a member of the team flapped a receipt at me nervously and asked, 'It's not worth claiming this back, though, is it? It's only £13.' £13! Of course she should claim it back, whether it's £13, £130 or 13p. Otherwise, how does anyone know the true cost? How can the home church support it? How will they enjoy the grace of giving to their Messy Church? And imagine the mortification your 'messy' congregation would feel if they discovered that their fun was at your personal expense—if they found out you had paid for their sausages yourself.

If you want to give to Messy Church as part of your offering to God, that's wonderful, but it is most effectively done through official channels, so that for every £1 you give, the church can claim another 22p (the rate at the time of writing) from HM Revenue and Customs. Giving regularly and efficiently like this also helps the team to plan a budget and add some extras that otherwise couldn't be afforded. If you have a separate bank account for Messy Church, you avoid having to claim money back through the church treasurer, who may not be around at Messy Church time. Cheques can be written there and then, before you lose the receipts.

I have to admit, I'm puzzled, as far as our budgeting goes. The home church has budgeted to pay £25 per month to Messy Church, but our treasurer says we haven't needed to claim any of it over the past year. Now, either the team is sneakily not claiming for what they spend, or we have extremely generous people putting in realistic donations, or God is providing mysteriously. It is very interesting that, in terms of direct spending, we seem to be independent of the church—although, of course, the use of the vicar, building, heat and light, along with the cost of wear and tear, is a huge hidden donation.

It is also worth considering the bigger picture: traditionally in the Church, children's work has been horrendously underfunded. There has been very little investment in children's work, in many churches, for many years. This under-investment has been one of the reasons why children have left the Church in droves. What does it say about your church if they are prepared to invest in outreach to the tune of just a few pounds a month—compared with how much might be spent on audiovisual multimedia gizmos, or flowers, or altar frontals? A big investment is symbolic as much as useful. Money is a sacrament, too! A significant investment says, 'We think this area of work is important. We believe in outreach. We desperately want these people to know Christ. We are putting our money where our mouth is. We will pay for this even though it means digging deeper in our pockets.' In 500 years' time, when archivists analyse the historic documents of your church, what will they deduce to be the church's main interest in the 21st century from the way the money is spent?

If you are thinking of starting, do plan a rough budget and get the church leadership to back you for double what you think it will cost to run Messy Church for six months. If your church is unable to support you, consider (after the obligatory rant at the church council about priorities, of course) charging an affordable amount per person per month.

The amount you will need to invest in Messy Church will depend upon the following factors, but the bigger question probably is, 'How much do you *want* to invest in Messy Church?' The basic outgoings will include:

✣ Publicity
✣ Number of meals to be provided (based on how many people you expect or can seat)
✣ Total cost of food for number of people

✣ Craft materials
✣ Craft equipment (one-off costs)
✣ Room hire

Reflect on your Messy Church
How much do you want to invest in Messy Church?

WHAT ABOUT PARENTS AND CARERS WHO WORK?

Alas, yes. It would be lovely to have Messy Church at a time when everyone could come. But, inevitably, whatever time you choose to have it, someone will be excluded. Later in the evening and it's too late for tinies and teens who have to do homework. At weekends, you lose out on those away for the weekend or doing sport. Working out when to hold your sessions is a huge issue that can only be decided at a very local level and will be different for all of us in our different situations. But if you have a midweek session that some parents or carers can't get to, how about copying what one Messy Church does and holding a fish 'n' chips 'n' quiz night every term on a Friday night, so that those who can't get to Messy Church because of work commitments can come along. Apparently, the evening is also a fundraiser for Messy Church, so not to be sniffed at.

WHAT DO YOU DO WHEN CHILDREN ARRIVE
WITHOUT AN ADULT?

It depends who they are. If they are children whom one of the team knows and trusts, and whose parents or carers we know, we make sure they know who is their 'responsible adult' for the session and we say that we need them to cooperate as we're very busy and can't go chasing after them if they're out of line. We also suggest that perhaps next time they could persuade their mum or grandad to come.

In our Messy Church, children arriving without an adult need to write down their phone numbers so that we have a contact in an emergency, and they are usually terribly helpful. If they are complete strangers, we find out if any of the adults present knows them and is prepared to be their responsible adult (which is usually the case). If they are a group of strangers known to nobody, we have to be a bit brutal and explain that they need a grown-up with them, suggesting that perhaps one of them could go home and collect a carer.

WHAT DO YOU DO WHEN ADULTS ARRIVE WITHOUT A CHILD?

We went through a stage in our own Messy Church, of discouraging 'unaccompanied adults' to come to Messy Church, fearing we might have child protection issues, or that people who hadn't been through our clearance system might be perceived as leaders when they were members of the congregation. I even included a paragraph in the first issue of this book to this effect. Since then we have changed our minds and come to understand that church isn't church unless it's open to everyone, so we welcome every adult who comes, keep our eyes open and enjoy the way people of all ages can be Messy Church together.

HOW DO YOU KEEP BOYS INTERESTED?

Well, it's not just the boys, of course, but this question is usually a short cut for saying, 'What about the kinaesthetic learners with short attention spans and an element of competitiveness and destructiveness in their make-up?' When we devise the crafts, we vet them to check that we have 'big' things to do as well as little finicky things. We try to have something construction-based, something chunky and thrown together rather than minutely pieced together at a table. Junk modelling is a good fall-back. Activities that involve an element of making and an element of competition are useful: making a paper plane and seeing whose flies furthest, blasting decorated bottles with a water pistol, building a den from cardboard —that sort of thing—and activities that include feet as well as hands. Also, food activities are always well received.

Some Messy Churches have begun offering computer activities as part of the craft session, on the grounds that there are plenty of creative programmes to explore both for their own sakes and to use as part of the celebration. Many computers, for example, have Windows Moviemaker and PowerPoint already installed, both of which can add an extra dimension to the celebration as well as being great fun to use.

WHAT ABOUT OLDER CHILDREN AND TEENAGERS?

We whisk them on to the leadership team as soon as they show an aptitude and yearning. Realistically, they will only keep coming while their younger siblings are coming, unless there is a peer group of teenagers who can lead crafts together and enjoy doing things as a group. One Messy Church in Derbyshire gives the whole job of organizing and leading the celebration to the youth team, who adapt and improve the ideas in the first *Messy Church* book beyond all recognition.

Loners can take photos of the crafts and download them on to the laptop or run a computer-based activity. Young people at that awkward 'too old to be seen to enjoy themselves but secretly still wanting to do crafts' stage can usefully take younger children round the activities and help them, to give carers a break, especially if the carers are the craft leaders.

Ideally, I would like to spend more time with our young leaders' team, giving them a sense of identity and purpose and exploring their ideas for developing Messy Church.

WHAT ABOUT CRB?

Before you start, get in touch with your child protection officer, find out what your local policy is and start the process as soon as possible. It can take longer than you think (someone who should be in our team has been sitting on their declaration forms for nine months now). The rule of thumb is that you will need CRB clearance for anyone who is in a leadership capacity of any sort.

IS IT REAL CHURCH?

Does Homer Simpson eat doughnuts? There's not space here to go into a detailed theological discussion about what constitutes church: you can find lots of interesting debate on the Fresh Expressions website and in many other places.

I've come to believe that what makes a difference is what you as a leadership group believe you are doing. If you think you are running a wholesome healthy-living club with a bit of singing thrown in, you will have a very different attitude to Messy Church from that of a group who believe they are building the body of Christ in their locality. The latter group will go through a lot more pain, soul-searching, hope, joy, awe and wonder than the first. It will cost more and it will be more of an adventure. It will offend more people and it will attract less money from outside funding. It will arouse stronger feelings and provoke more questions than it answers. It will have a dynamism that will be hard to explain. It will matter more. I wonder how you would answer this question in your context: 'If your Messy Church were to fold at the end of the year, would it matter?'

Reflect on your Messy Church
How much does being church matter? How much does Messy Church matter?

49

CHAPTER 5

Food

Let's talk about food—a subject dear to my heart. One of the challenges and attractions of Messy Church is its emphasis on eating together. It is well worth reflecting on why we go to all the angst of peeling a thousand potatoes, frying up dozens of packs of mince, chopping endless cucumbers and grating cheese till the RSI comes home. Why do we bother, when we know it's going to make piles of washing-up and leave us with that depressing tray of soggy half-burnt leftovers to take home and feel depressed about eating but guilty about throwing away? When it costs so much and our budget is so tight? When half the children moan that they don't like anything with fish/meat/vegetables/rice in, and the parents make knowing comments about E-numbers in the cake colouring? After all, very few, if any, of those attending Messy Church actually need us to provide food as if we were a soup kitchen. Surely it would be easier, cheaper and more manageable to send everyone home after some craft and worship?

Yes it would.

But eating together is an element of Messy Church that is so precious that we need to grasp what we are actually doing when we sit and eat with people in Jesus' name. We're not just stuffing roughage and protein into digestive tracts, any more than the *Mona Lisa* is just some blobs of oil paint on a bit of canvas. Something bigger is going on—and we're going back several thousand years to an ancient story to try to understand what it is.

You'll find the story in Genesis 18:1–15. Sarah and her husband Abraham are nomads, pitching their tent in the desert for as long as they find pasture for their flocks, then upping sticks and wandering on

50

to a new site. They are living in tents, travelling with servants, extended family and animals—a community on the hoof, responsive to the world around them, pretty much self-sufficient. But, prosperous though they are, the wild space in which they are wandering is inhospitable, and someone on their own out there in the wilderness wouldn't survive for very long.

So, in a desert country, you keep an eye open for other people in need and, knowing that it might one day be you or your children in dire straits, you treat a stranger as an honoured guest. You feed them first and ask questions later. Also, who knows what news this stranger might have? What stories of kings and crimes, of the farflung tribes probably related to you via your mother's cousin's great-aunt's nephew's father's daughter, that you can find out no other way, the Internet not having reached your tent yet?

Abraham and Sarah are elderly and carry round with them a raw wound and a healing promise. They have no children of their own. (There is Ishmael, but he isn't Sarah's child and his existence makes the situation even more painful.) But God has promised Abraham that one day they will have a child together, who will somehow be the way God's blessing will be spilled out on to the whole earth. It's just past lunch time. Abraham is settling down for a siesta in his tent and casts a lazy practised eye over the shimmering landscape. Then he blinks. His sight must be failing more than he realized. Apparently out of nowhere, there are three figures standing nearby. Abraham rushes out to them, bows low and invites them to lunch there in the shade of the trees. They accept, and he scuttles off to mobilize the forces: Sarah is set to making bread, a servant is given a calf to prepare and Abraham gets out the milkshakes.

The three strangers eat their meal, then one of them asks for Sarah and says that this time next year he'll be coming back and by that time she'll have a son. Sarah is eavesdropping behind her tent flap and has a derisive internal chuckle at the thought of anyone having a baby when they are as elderly as she is. Cocoa is probably as exciting as it gets in Sarah's sleeping bag these days. But the stranger insists (in fact, the narrator has slipped into calling him 'the Lord' by now).

He asks why Sarah laughed and reminds them that nothing is impossible for God.

By now, Sarah has crept out from her tent to defend herself with the lie, 'I didn't laugh' (unwittingly saying the name of her son-to-be in a Hebrew anagram), and the Lord finishes off, 'Yes, you did laugh.' When the story is told round campfires to Sarah's grandchildren and great-grandchildren, you can imagine this ending turning into an 'Oh no, I didn't!' 'Oh yes, you did!' riot of laughter. A year later, of course, Isaac is born.

OK—tents, deserts, angels, yoghurt and thousands of years ago. What has this got to say to the hubbub of ketchup and pasta that faces you every month? This passage is one of those beautifully constructed classic stories that opens up and up and up the more you look at it, and leaves you going, 'Oh *yes*, and what about…?' as it rings bells in all sorts of directions, especially as we look at what Messy Church is all about—outreach and deepening faith.

Think about these ideas while you wait for your own to pop up.

OASIS

I was lucky enough to go by plane on a short-haul flight the other day. Flying above the clouds, it was like being perched on a (admittedly, rather tall) camel riding across a desert: the cloudscape was full of beauty but there were no points of reference in it; everything was shifting and inconstant. We could have been anywhere and it was utterly disorientating. To strangers in the desert, Abraham and Sarah's encampment must have seemed like a welcome, solid, stable point in the middle of the shifting sands of their environment.

Do people around you live in a state of uncertainty, with shifts and changes happening all around them? Are they anxious at a very deep level because the old certainties are gone and there's nothing stable and solid in their lives any more? You can put it down to many causes: the dizzying advances in technology; the devastating unreliability of once-permanent relationships; the lack of trust, especially of authority;

the constant questioning of a postmodern (or post-post-postmodern) society that takes nothing as a given. Can your church provide an oasis of stability for travellers in these shifting sands? A place of safety and refuge; a place to ask questions without being rejected; a place to go out from, refreshed and reinvigorated, with trust renewed and a new sense of direction?

Messy Church, like all good churches, is an oasis where strangers can find refuge from a hostile world, feel welcomed and respected, find their feet in their own time and go away feeling refreshed and resourced to cope with the struggles of the onward journey.

Reflect on your Messy Church
Is your church an oasis or a continuation of the desert?

SIESTA

Abraham was elderly, surrounded by servants. At this point in the immediate story, he was just about to have a siesta. In the long term, also, he was waiting in faith, but without any idea how or when God's promise to make his family a great nation would be kept.

Does your church ever feel as if everyone's having a siesta? Sitting back and putting their feet up, leaving the work to someone else? How many times have you heard, 'Oh I've done my bit. It's the youngsters' turn to make the coffee/cook the parish Christmas meal/ organize the Easter egg hunt. It's someone else's turn to do the work.' Or maybe, worse still, the fulfilment of God's promise and vision for your church and area has been so long in coming that people have forgotten about them and lost the excitement they once had. One Messy Church team I visited shared a tale of waiting as a church: they had been praying and seeking the way forward with children and young people for years—literally years—before they came across this particular form of outreach and saw the possibilities for their families. How easy it would have been for them to lose heart in the waiting time, and to give up on ever seeing God moving.

There is no hint in this story that Abraham begrudges the loss of his siesta. On the contrary, he leaps off his bed, runs out of the cool of his tent and into the scorching midday sun to welcome the visitors. This is no Eastern potentate, snapping his fingers at minions to do the work, although he does delegate efficiently to organize Sarah and the servants. Abraham is a vigorous, independent self-starter who takes responsibility for his own community. Unlike Martha and Mary, who polarized work versus listening to God, Abraham combines the hard work of a host with a gracious stillness as he waits on his guests. It's as if he doesn't see it as drudgery; rather it is his privilege and joy to welcome these outsiders. He has the flexibility of time and resources in his lifestyle to drop everything to attend to what is most important. He takes pride in being the one to be able to invite them in.

Outreach is something all ages can play a part in—building on the skills of older generations as well as younger, bringing new life, direction, dignity and energy to people who can use their cooking / craft / listening skills to welcome outsiders into a church community. It is a job that requires us to work as hard as kitchen skivvies, to listen and watch like waiters, and to do it all happily without resentment. It is a joy to hear again and again of the way older and younger church members are working together at crafts and in kitchens to share Jesus' love with families who don't yet know him.

Reflect on your Messy Church
Who are your Abrahams?

LAUGHTER

This story is surrounded with laughter, through the woman and through the promise of the child (as Isaac actually means 'laughter').

Laughter is a sign of the kingdom, and we should be hearing it in our church communities, in counterpoint to the weeping and pain this side of heaven. I suspect that the Gospel writers don't ever mention Jesus laughing simply because he was laughing all the time and it would have got tedious to mention it. It is impossible to think of Jesus giving the painful, bitter, disillusioned internal chuckle that Sarah does (unless it was at the antics of some of the Pharisees), but then Jesus had the big picture clear in his head and Sarah was stuck in years of painful waiting for a baby.

'Where is Sarah?' The question has powerful overtones of something monumental about to happen, like 'Where are you, Adam?' or 'Where is your brother Abel?' It reminds us that we need to keep asking where people are, miss them when they're away, notice them as friends and brothers and sisters, reaffirm their identity as children of God, and keep on renewing the relationship, especially with people like Sarah, who may be feeling they don't count. Many young mums are going through a crisis of identity, having given up a job to look after an unappreciative baby. Loneliness kicks in so quickly. As we build up 'messy' communities, let's keep asking, 'Where is...?'

It's very telling that Sarah assumes that life has passed her by— that an ordinary, everyday, human desire (for Sarah, that of being a mother) is not to be. God delights in our delight in ordinary, everyday things: creating, painting, singing, eating, drinking, talking, making. These aren't the icing on the cake of a worshipful life. They *are* worship; they are sanctified, sacramental acts. Enjoying everyday things means that God breaks out of a 'one day in seven is holy' prison and bubbles up in the whole of our lives, bursting into our classrooms, offices and gyms. We should encourage people to rediscover pleasure in ordinary wholesome acts in our church worship and community life. We should demonstrate how hallowed they are by enjoying everyday things together as church. Just as 'laughter' in this story is inextricably tied up with a child, we need children among us to show us the way: undamaged children are the experts at enjoying the everyday miracles of life. I hope, if our Messy

Church ever meets an angel, to us he'll insist like the Lord did to Sarah, 'Yes, you did laugh!'

Reflect on your Messy Church
How much do you expect people to *enjoy* being together as church?

THE MEAL

Food is the central point of this story, a story that influences and informs other Bible stories as well as how we eat together today. The story of the three visitors is very exciting in all its echoes: think especially of a story told by Jesus, where someone rushes out in undignified haste to greet a visitor, welcomes him in, throws a feast for him with the very best that he has to offer (in fact, with another fatted calf) and where the feast itself is both a healing of family breakdown and a point of tension between old and new relationships. Think of the time after Jesus' resurrection, when a meal revealed who he was.

God has made us to need food. He has made food fun. He has made sharing food an opportunity to meet and know each other and to meet and know him, in some mysterious way that many of us don't fully understand. We call this sort of rite a sacrament.

A sacrament is variously defined (or described) as a visible sign of an inward grace—something regarded as possessing a sacred character or mysterious significance; a symbolic action. It's something you can see, but it is more than what you can see, and that 'more than' is full of some aspect of God. Certainly, in the Abraham story in Genesis 18:1–15, the food that Abraham chooses for an ordinary meal—the best bull, the measures of wheat flour—has overtones of sacrificial food, food set apart for God. I would suggest that it is only by doing the ordinary action that we can hope to get a glimpse of the extraordinary supernatural wonderfulness of God behind it.

In our (Sunday) church, which is Anglican, we usually use the word 'sacrament' in the context of the Eucharist or baptisms—both very 'churchy' services. But perhaps we need to recover the ordinariness to rediscover the holy. Are we worshipping at a Eucharist? Are we worshipping at Messy Church tea time? Is one holier than the other? Does God use one more powerfully than the other? Do we meet him, are we healed, restored and resourced by him, at one more than at the other? Do we recognize him more fully at one because we met him at the other? These aren't rhetorical questions: they are significant ones to ask, because it takes a great deal of work to get that meal on the table and it is worth analysing why we do it. And no, I don't know the answers! I'm still getting my head round it all.

We included the meal within Messy Church really because we couldn't face going home and having to cook tea for our own families after the stress of 'mess'. It wasn't a thought-through, theological ordinance. And yet it has somehow been one of the main aspects of Messy Church that gives it identity: it has been the part that other churches have seized upon as a good idea. It's almost as if we all knew instinctively that eating together as a church community is right, but we needed someone to say, 'Go for it! You can do it!'

Meal times

So what are we doing when we eat together? Why is the meal time of Messy Church, or any other gathering for food, more than just a bun fight?

Let's leave Abraham for a moment and go forward in time to Jesus. What did he think of meals? His culture, of course, was very different from ours. Meal times were important for Jewish communities to an extent that is hard for us, in the Christianized and rationalized West, to grasp. In the Gospels there's a background of open-handed hospitality and friendship around tables, which doesn't even get a mention because it was as obvious as saying, 'Jesus got up in the morning.' So, where food is mentioned up front, it is significant.

Plunge with me into just one of the Gospels. To put some sort of limit on what could be a thesis in itself, let's look at Luke's Gospel. Luke is a writer who notices food, and, as he builds up a picture of Jesus, he uses meals to show Jesus... doing what? Well, building community, welcoming outsiders and deepening discipleship and relationships. Whoop! Just what we are trying to do in our Messy Churches! Luke builds up a picture of food, not to make the case that 'you are what you eat', but to demonstrate that 'you are who you eat with' and 'you are how you eat'.

There we find meals which are about bodily sustenance, about a very human need for food and dependency on God for that food, such as Jesus' suggestion to give some food to Jairus' daughter after bringing her back from the dead (Luke 8:55), the feeding of the five thousand (9:13), and the request for daily bread in the Lord's Prayer (11:3). Eating together is a simple, fundamental human need which is also, by the grace of God, a pleasure, available to anyone from birth to the end of life. What bliss to bite into a warm, fragrant, crumbly bun or to let your taste buds weep for joy over a sliver of smoked salmon. It's something we are blessed enough to enjoy every day and it is worth bringing it into the church sphere, if only to remind everyone that our everyday food, in and out of church, comes from God. If we are trying to provide an impetus for people to start recognizing and appreciating God in their homes, a meal is a good place to start in church.

Then there are the meals which highlight the fact that food stands for something spiritual, such as Jesus' temptation to turn stones into bread (Luke 4:3), the feeding of the five thousand, with its echoes of the food in the wilderness during the exodus (9:16), or the ambiguity of the prayer 'Give us today our daily bread' (11:3). Perhaps eating sausage and mash as a church is a first step towards a deeper understanding of the Eucharist. All the thinking about all-age church indicates that it is impossible to have an all-age service unless you have an all-age community, with all its relationships of love and acceptance threading the body together in the background.

Eating, say, jacket potatoes together teaches everyone something of the need for order, the enjoyment of companionship, the different speeds at which people eat, the different ways people enjoy their food, and the different things they get out of it. Lesley always makes flapjack but, on one occasion, she didn't think she needed to as we had a superabundance of buns. There was a wail of anguish from a three-year-old who had been looking forward to his flapjack all through Messy Church. Buns were not an adequate substitute. I had never had any idea how precious flapjack was to him, or how important a ritual it was. I find it hard to appreciate the Eucharist myself, but this child's outburst reminded me how all-important the bread and wine are to others, in a way I haven't properly begun to explore for myself, and how I need to respect that in them. Eating helps us to become a body, bigger than just ourselves.

There are meals that show something about grace, about demonstrating love by showing hospitality to the loved one, like Simon's mother-in-law's meal (Luke 4:39), the anointing of Jesus by a woman at a dinner party (7:38), contrasted with the lack of welcome shown by Simon the Pharisee (vv. 44–45), and Martha and Mary's meal (10:38–42). Children are often devastatingly welcoming to the adult leaders at the Messy Church meal, saving us places, insisting that we sit next to them, making it obvious how much they value our company. It is very humbling and shows something about the circular grace of giving: adults make generous donations to enable us to buy food; we provide tea, and the children respond by giving us unconditional love. Olivia kept her beady eye on me as I staggered in from a busy 'messy' celebration to a crowded hall of people already eating, and vigorously patted the seat beside her, a huge grin on her face—a holy moment.

There are meals that are celebrations of community, of the lost being found and returned to the family, like Levi (Luke 5:29), Zacchaeus (19:7) and the people involved in the 'lost' parables (15:6, 9, 24). In 'messy' meals we are celebrating our identity as a family of lost and found. We are demonstrating our welcome of everyone, regardless of age and ability. During the meal the other week, we became aware of a couple of dads and a husband lurking furtively in the church hallway, just back from work, waiting for their families to finish eating. It was great to welcome them in, find space for them near their loved ones and plonk large platefuls of chicken korma in front of them. No one has to earn their right to a meal by taking a course or passing an exam. This is an open community, which gives because we recognize that Jesus gave so much to us first.

There are Jesus' parables which use food to express something of the kingdom: the rich fool stockpiling and abusing food (Luke 12:16–20), the woman with the measures of flour (like Sarah!) (13:20–21), the great banquet to which all are invited (14:15–24), and the rich man who refuses to share bread or meat with Lazarus (16:19–31). Each one of these stories could have reams written about it in this context, but they certainly give us some useful reminders: the parable of the rich fool and his barns, and the parable of the rich man and Lazarus, say something about our use and abuse of church resources. How much are we, who have all the riches of heaven at our fingertips, prepared to use what we have got for people who don't belong? One Messy Church (not ours) faced the issue of a church treasurer who demanded to know when all these new people were going to start contributing towards the parish share (the contribution that the Anglican parishes make towards the work of the wider diocese).

The yeast in the flour reminds us about God's pattern of working, which is to take our small efforts and turn them into something exciting and new. It is also a good reminder that we can pile up all the flour we've got—we can plough all the money and time we like into Messy Church—but unless there's the yeast of God's Spirit mixed into every aspect of what we are doing, it will stay lumpy and useless. We need to keep praying and actively involving God at every moment.

The parable of the great banquet reminds us about the way we can help people look forward to heaven's party by getting into practice with the celebration now. It is also a reminder to keep the doors open and never to exclude unlikely people (other than with the caveat mentioned on page 47). Obviously, we have a slight issue that the master of the banquet didn't have: we have to comply with child protection requirements, which makes it difficult to extend a welcome to people who want to attend without children, especially if they are Sunday church members who haven't been CRB cleared (again, see page 47). But the principle remains: Messy Church is church for people who don't go to church. This is a party for people who don't get invited to parties, certainly not parties where they can come together as a family.

Some meals in Luke's Gospel are the setting for scenes of conflict between Jesus and the establishment: again, at Levi's house, and at the home of a Pharisee (Luke 5:30; 11:37–44); in the fields, as eating corn reveals attitudes about the sabbath laws (6:2); at the dinner party where Jesus is anointed (7:39); and at the home of Martha and Mary, where Mary chooses 'the better way' above Martha's traditional female role of hostess (10:41–42). Meals reveal something that is going on under the surface: they are symbolic.

Perhaps we can expect the meal time to be a focus for flare-ups as well as friendship. One person from our Messy Church, who also comes to Sunday church, used to bring her grandchild along. When we asked why she no longer came, she said she was worried that the lack of table manners shown by some of the children there would send the wrong message to her grandchild. It was an understandable reaction from a fond grandmother, but showed a complete lack of understanding of the bigger picture of our aim, which is a long-term process of gently setting standards that will make everyone comfortable at the table together, not insisting on middle-class table manners being learnt, or excluding rude people. She didn't see that she could help improve the situation by being there as a good influence, rather than simply disappearing from the scene.

Finally, of course, we look back at the early Church in Acts, who no doubt ate together. Would you say that eating together has been a sign of the Church since then? If you ask schoolchildren about faith and food, they might tell you about Sikh hospitality, where it's unthinkable not to offer a visitor food. They might talk about food used for celebrating religious festivals, like turkey at Christmas. They might even, at a push, mention Holy Communion. But, if eating together—ordinary everyday eating together—is a sign of the kingdom community, why hasn't it been pivotal to church development over the centuries? Why is it strange for most churches to eat together, apart from soggy biscuits after the service and harvest suppers? Why is the Alpha supper still an exception to the run of church life, rather than the rule? Is Messy Church, as much as anything, another chance to recapture this fun and holy act and to put table companionship right at the heart of church life? Wouldn't it be great if you asked children what they do at church and they replied, 'We all enjoy eating together'?

Is the 'messy' meal sacramental?

In Luke's Gospel, there is the meal that links all these themes together with its intimacy, its richness of symbolism and sacrament, its unity and conflict, its celebration and remembrance, its reaching back to the past and its looking to the future—the Lord's Supper (22:14–19), with its echo in the meal at Emmaus (24:13–35).

There is, of course, a fundamental difference between a 'messy' meal and a Holy Communion, in that the Eucharist is a specific reminder of Jesus' death and resurrection, whereas 'messy' meals in general are much more about celebrating God's goodness and grace, our shared love for each other as his children and our enjoyment of being part of the kingdom of heaven. Obviously, it would be inappropriate to ask people to substitute shepherd's pie for the elements of Holy Communion, but it is entirely appropriate to ask them to say 'thank you' to God for the shepherd's pie that he's provided out of his great goodness for us. The 'messy' meal and the bread and wine are doing different things, but point towards the same loving Jesus in ways that speak to people at different points on their journey of faith. Perhaps we will arrive at a better understanding of the one after enjoying the other.

After much thought, and encouraged by the understanding that the Eucharist itself can help people along the discipleship journey, I have included a suggested outline for a Communion celebration (see pages 208–210). Depending on your denomination, you may need to check with the appropriate authorities that it is OK to use it in your context. You may want to quote from Bishop Lindsay Urwin, in his chapter on the role of sacramental ministry in Fresh Expressions, where he writes about the need to deregulate the sacraments.

We need to consider 'chilling out' with regard to the rules and regulations with which we steward [the sacraments], so that they may be the blessing they truly are... [An experience of the sacraments used in a fresh expression] underlines for me the need in sacramental fresh expressions to have a 'lively doctrine of exceptions'.[1]

I was delighted to hear from our own bishop that he, too, is very much in favour of our not getting too hung up on words and precise liturgy, but instead being part of the story of Holy Communion that has been shaped, changed and adapted over the centuries. In Portsmouth, Messy Church will be part of a diocesan think tank to work out how we can best and most appropriately offer this wonderful gift to the different people who come to our churches, especially those on the fringe. We did wonder about simply holding an *agape* meal rather than wrestling with the intricacies of Holy Communion itself. This would avoid worries about acceptable liturgy and would help people to experience something of the last supper. But our feeling was that if we are serious about being church, if this congregation has as much right as the Sunday church to all the 'proper' forms of celebration, we should make an effort to offer them the best we can. For us in this context, it meant a eucharistic service. In your situation you might arrive at a very different conclusion.

I do believe that in Fresh Expressions we need to be more open in our approach to Holy Communion and to think imaginatively about what it means for people who are following Christ within a Fresh Expressions context to meet him in the sacraments.

It is my understanding that Holy Communion is a gift from God to help us come close to him. It isn't a wage packet to be earnt, a hoop to jump through or a course to help us know all the right answers. The Eucharist is a mysterious way of coming close to God, not a prize for being right with him. If we are to be shaped by our mission, and work from outsiders in, I would argue that we need to offer this gift to our Messy Church people so that, when they are ready, they can fall in love with God through it and arrive at a point where they want to walk closer with him.

The suggested celebration outline on pages 208–210 is simple. It focuses on getting ready to draw near to God through the sacrament and, through the sacrament, being ready to go back out into the world filled with his love. Bishop Lindsay writes again: 'We need to demystify the mystery, making it easier for people to enter the mystery, rather than dumb it down.'[2]

The responses are predictable and simple, so you shouldn't need any service orders or even words on a screen. The outline also uses the Messy Church structure to enrich the actual celebration. For example, the crafts you make beforehand can be used in the celebration, which will help everyone to feel personally involved and contributing—just as Jesus' disciples prepared the room for the Passover meal. The Bible exploration happens not just in the celebration with the retelling of the story of the last supper, but also in the crafts. Finally, we collect all our worship together with the familiar 'messy' grace, to lead us on our way laughing into teatime.

Just after Easter 2008, we held our first Messy Communion after a great deal of prayer, heartache and discussion, as we tried to balance the needs of our 'messy' congregation with the requirements of the Anglican Church to which we belong. It was a surprisingly moving occasion. We didn't get everything right first time, but nonetheless it was something that felt very right and, at some fundamental level, we feel it has shifted us forwards on our faith journey as a community. The celebration featured aspects that helped it to feel informal yet reverent, friendly yet tapping into an 'otherness' or 'mystery', satisfying but question-provoking. Here are some of the features that stood out:

✤ The invitation to hold someone's hand as we went into church, so that no one was left out, said something profound about our togetherness.

✤ The repeated questioning 'Are you ready?' before we went into the church fulfilled the same function as the question asked of people joining a *Godly Play* story circle: it helped people to prepare for something different, to cross a threshold.

✤ The loose circle in which we stood around the table for the whole service gave a visible sense of unity and equality.

✤ The lack of printed words not only made us all equal but helped us focus on the centrality of the bread and wine.

✤ The cup and plate had been made beforehand and prayers had been prayed during the craft time and written on leaves hung on a prayer tree, which were all brought into the church, placed on the table and commented on. Our activities outside the celebration were thus drawn into the celebration itself: the 'secular' and 'sacred' were undivided.

✤ We took the line, 'If you are confirmed, or take Holy Communion, in your own church, please have the bread and the wine; if you aren't yet confirmed, please have a blessing.' A few of the children tried for the bread but admitted bashfully that they didn't usually have it and seemed happy with a blessing. It was very equalizing: some of the adults took bread and wine; some didn't; some of the children did and some didn't.

✤ Some of the people present had probably never been prayed for personally before, and the 'formal' blessing was an ideal way of praying for them without embarrassing them. Some people didn't know what a blessing is.

✤ The event provoked a lot of questions from the children during teatime afterwards and should lead on to a natural way forward in discipleship as we consider an all-age 'preparation for Communion before confirmation' type of course.

Jesus died and rose again for everyone, not just his disciples. He left them a symbolic act that could be shared and understood at many different levels, but that would also enrich discipleship at any stage of life. Our task is to make sure we don't get in God's way, in enabling others to share in this mysterious and holy act.

Reflect on your Messy Church
Jesus said, 'Let the children come to me! Don't try to stop them. People who are like these children belong to God's kingdom' (Luke 18:16). Do we really believe that?

Here is Bishop Lindsay's concluding paragraph.

There is a desperate need in the fresh expression movement to nudge the Church and especially those in leadership, to both rediscover the possibility of an encounter with Jesus in sacramental events and to enable the experience in new ways, for the sake not only of those who do not yet believe, but to rekindle the desire in existing believers. There is a need for de-regulation in evangelistic circumstances, for a proper and agreed doctrine of exceptions as we seek to draw in to life with Christ those who are so far from us and who do not realise the source of their hunger. Jesus has food to give and only he can provide it. We are his providers and if we fail to feed in his name, we will answer.[3]

Let's go back to Abraham and Sarah. The meal in the desert is a pattern for us in our Messy Churches. We don't know who we are welcoming to our tables; we may well be entertaining angels unawares. When we look at the people coming in, do we look for and honour Christ in them—the holy in the ordinary? It's hard work (and team work) to prepare the meal, but something inside us recognizes the rightness of welcoming the stranger with food and drink.

When we receive people to our church home in Jesus' name, we are shouting a countercultural message of hospitality and are offering respite and refreshment to those passing through. It is around a meal that the Lord reveals himself. It is also around a meal that our identities are reinforced as children of the same heavenly Father, as people who are named, loved, needed and significant. It is at a meal that God renews his promise to Abraham's family and to us, his church family, a promise that is not just a blessing for the immediate gathering of people, but one that will continue to heap blessings on generations to come and on the community around the church, through children and family life. In just the same way, the birth of Isaac was the tiny start of something amazing and unpredictable.

It may be a sad, despairing, barren, waiting time for your church, just as Sarah was reduced to wry despair as she waited for a child, hoping against hope for new life. But, around our Messy Church tables, we can all enjoy the Spirit's renewing energy, excitement, hope for the future and purpose in the present. We can laugh together again.

Notes
1 *Mission-Shaped Questions* (Church House Publishing, 2008), pp. 29, 35.
2 *Mission-Shaped Questions*, p. 31.
3 *Mission-Shaped Questions*, p. 41.

CHAPTER 6

Menu ideas

I've given up on numbers, as my maths is appalling, I'm relentlessly imperial rather than metric, everyone is dealing with different numbers and it's impossible to judge anyway. I'm sure you can work it all out! And do keep checking the Messy Church website, www.messychurch.org.uk, for new recipe ideas that people are kind enough to send us or give us at Messy Fiestas.

SAVOURY DISHES

Chicken or quorn korma

Cook chicken pieces and pour over a ready-made korma sauce (from a jar). Serve with rice, vegetables and poppadoms.

Ploughperson's tea

On each plate put a slab of cheese, half an apple, a wodge of cucumber and a roll or a chunk of French bread. Have pickle and pickled onions available for people to help themselves.

Sausage casserole

Brown the sausages in a grill or frying pan and chop them into slices or chunks. Add tins of butter beans. Soften sliced onions and add to the sausages. Pour over a stock or gravy and mixed herbs and cook until the sausages are piping hot and cooked all the way through. Serve with mashed potato and vegetables or baked beans. Use veggie sausages as an alternative.

French bread pizza

Slice baguette loaves open lengthways and top them with tomato sauce, grated cheese and different toppings, such as peppers, salami, ham or pineapple. Serve with cucumber slices and carrot sticks.

Soup sauce casserole

Spread out turkey pieces (and sliced vegetables, if desired) in casserole dishes. Pour tins of condensed soup over them (mushroom or chicken soups are ideal). Cook for about an hour. Have a quorn or mushroom soup option for vegetarians. If you are being posh, you could bake some star shapes out of puff pastry and deposit one on top of each serving (however, 80 puffy stars in an unpredictable oven nearly drove poor Clare to drink).

Pitta pockets

Make up a basic mince-based sauce and fill a pitta pocket with it. Serve with cucumber or carrot sticks.

Hotdogs and wedges

This worked nicely when we had a summer Messy Church picnic tea in the garden. Hot dogs, salady bits, ketchup, finger rolls… For the wedges, slice up potatoes into wedges, boil for five minutes or so, pour over some oil and garlic if you like and give them a good oily shake. Bake in a really hot oven for about 40 minutes.

Pasta twirls with tomato sauce

It is easiest to make this by using ready-made pasta sauces (from a jar). Serve with French bread and grated cheese, cucumber and cold sweetcorn in bowls on the tables so that people can help themselves.

BISCUITS AND BREAD

Gingerbread biscuits

You will need: 300g plain flour, a pinch of salt, 1 tsp baking powder, 1 tsp ground ginger, 100g butter or margarine, 100g soft brown sugar, 2 eggs, 60g golden syrup, mixing bowl, mixing spoon or hand-held mixer, baking parchment or greaseproof paper, flour, mini chocolate or candy sweets, or currants

Put the flour, salt, baking powder and spice into a bowl. Rub in the butter or margarine, then stir in the sugar. Beat the eggs with the golden syrup and add to the mixture. Mix well either by hand or with a hand-held mixer. **NB:** Make sure people wash their hands before the activity.

Divide the mixture into pieces sufficient for each person. Have a surface ready for rolling, such as pieces of well-floured baking parchment or greaseproof paper on your normal table covering. The mixture should be rolled out to about 5mm thickness and then the biscuits can be cut out with people-shaped cutters. Decorate with mini chocolate or candy sweets or currants. Place each biscuit on a square of baking parchment, marked with the person's name, then put the biscuits on a baking sheet and bake them in an oven pre-heated to Gas Mark 4 or 160°C for about 18 minutes.

NB: As the biscuit recipe has egg in it, make sure people don't eat the raw mixture.

Bread dough

You will need: 400g strong plain flour, 2 level tsp sugar, 2 level tsp dried yeast (the easy baking variety), 230ml plus 5 tbsp warm water, 1.5 level tsp salt, 2 tbsp olive oil, two mixing bowls, mixing spoon, sieve, clean tea towel, greaseproof paper

Sift the flour, sugar, yeast and salt into a bowl (if you are using yeast that needs to be reconstituted in water first, follow the instructions on the packet). Add the oil and water and knead well. Cover with a clean tea towel and leave in a warm place for approximately one hour until double in size. Turn out on to a floured surface and knead again evenly until smooth. Divide the dough and shape as required. Place the items on a greased and floured baking tray. Cover with the tea towel and leave until doubled in size.

Bake in the centre of an oven at Gas Mark 5 or 190°C for 45–50 minutes for a loaf and 15–20 minutes for rolls, until the top is golden brown and the base sounds hollow when tapped. Cool on a wire rack.

MESSY GRACE

Invite everyone to hold three fingers in the air. Turning your hand round 180 degrees with each number and putting your fingers up or down to go with the numbers, say: '3, 2, 1; 1, 2, 3; thank you, God, for our tea.'

Thematic programmes

All the songs (unless otherwise stated) are taken from
The Doug Horley Humungous Songbook
(Children's Ministry, 2005).

UNIT 1

Love God!

This unit is one in a series on loving God, loving your neighbour and loving your world.

AIM

To encourage people to see God as a loving parent.

BIBLE BACKGROUND (Luke 15:11–32)

The parable of the two sons

What better way to think about the abstract idea of loving God than through the very concrete story often known as 'the prodigal son'— even though, arguably, the real thrust of the story isn't about the prodigal (extravagant) spending of the younger boy but either the response of the older boy or the attitude of the father. This parable is one that can be read in many different ways and, although the questions suggested at the end of the celebration story focus on the father, you will probably find that comments on the sons come up too.

FOOD

Farm food

Jacket potatoes, ham, cheese, baked beans and a touch of cucumber. (We considered fatted calf but had objections on animal welfare grounds—even more on price.)

ACTIVITIES

Pigs in the pen

You will need: Rich Tea biscuits, green and red food colouring, fondant icing, Matchmaker chocolate sticks

Decorate a biscuit with a layer of green fondant icing for the grass (or brown if you want to be more bestial) upon which are arranged Matchmaker chocolate sticks to form a pig pen. Make up some pink fondant icing and mould into pig shapes to put in the pen. The creativity comes with the structure of the pen and the design and detail of the pigs. If desired, people can colour their own icing.

Talk about
During this activity, talk about the mess animals make.

Tears of God

You will need: Clear acetate, OHP pens, clear thread, a cross in a pot, a hole punch

Make a tear-shaped template and use it to cut out the shape from acetate sheets. Invite people to draw or write on the acetate (using

OHP pens) what they think makes God cry. Punch a hole in the narrow end with a hole punch and use transparent thread to hang the tears from the crossbar of a cross. (The one we had was about two feet high and was held upright in a large flowerpot filled with stones.)

Talk about
During this activity, talk about what makes God sad.

Cocktails

You will need: A selection of weird and wonderful fruit juices and some fizzy water, plus plastic glasses, swizzler sticks, straws, cherries, ice cubes, little umbrellas or whatever the budget allows

Design, name and drink your own fruity cocktail.

Talk about
During this activity, talk about parties. There must have been plenty of parties in the parable of the two sons when the younger son was indulging in 'wild living' in a faraway land. And, of course, there is the party thrown by the dad to welcome back his errant son.

Pigswill

You will need: Jelly, clean bucket, food items as below

Make up several pints of jelly and pour it into a clean bucket. In the jelly, plant various items such as hardboiled eggs, a lump of cooked pasta, a bread roll, a slice of pizza or anything else you can find that's rather revolting. The object is to feel into the pigswill and guess what the object you've found might be and, of course, to pull it out and go 'Uuuuurgh!' at it before you put it back for the next person to find.

Talk about
During this activity, talk about being hungry. How hungry would you have to be to eat what you find in this bucket?

Farm collage

> **You will need:** A prepared display board, black sugar paper, scissors, PVA glue, party accessories such as streamers, balloons and other party novelties

Put a simple farm silhouette on the display board. Stick on the party accessories to make it look as if a great party is happening inside. Title: Welcome Home!

Talk about
During this activity, talk about parties.

Coin rubbing

> **You will need:** a selection of coins to rub with wax crayons, paper (optional: card, scissors, PVA glue)

You can find out how to rub brass properly on the Monumental Brass Society website (www.mbs-brasses.co.uk), or just put some paper over the coins and scribble. Done carefully, these rubbings look very attractive mounted on card backgrounds.

Talk about

During this activity, talk about where money comes from: pocket money, a job, presents, being left it in a will, and so on.

String hearts

You will need: Card, string, paint

Cut out a nice big heart from light cardboard. Dip a piece of string into some paint and drop it or drag it on the heart to leave a painty trail. Repeat with as many colours as you like, experimenting with different lengths of string. The finished heart is bright and beautiful.

Talk about

During this activity, talk about love: who you love, who loves you, God's love for everyone, different sorts of love and so on.

Junk farm

You will need: A large sheet of card (optional), scraps of coloured card, a good supply of sticky tape, PVA glue, scissors and junk including fake fur scraps and wool oddments

Either encourage people to make one huge junk farm together with barns, animals, machines, fields, ponds and so on, or to make an animal or farm machine on their own to take home. (The second option does mean you don't have the problem of what to do with six square metres of beautiful but messy junk at the end.)

Talk about
During this activity, talk about farms you have visited.

Trinity banner

You will need: An artistic person, a sheet of card, funky art foam or scraps of fabric, PVA glue or needles and thread, scissors

Over the next three Messy Church sessions, you might like to have an ongoing project to make a banner, completing one part each month. As the series is called 'Love God, love your neighbour, love your world', divide a banner background into three parts and fill one section during each session. The first, for 'Love God', could be triangles of different sizes and colours to represent the three persons of the Trinity. Cut the triangles from funky art foam or scraps of fabric and glue or sew them on to the banner.

Talk about
During this activity, talk about the Trinity.

Pencil top parable

You will need: Pipe cleaners, felt, foam, googly eyes, PVA glue, scissors, pencils

The boy in today's story goes away from home for a while. Perhaps he wrote letters home while he was away, or maybe his dad wrote him letters (the Bible doesn't mention the boy's mother). Use felt scraps or coloured pipe cleaners to design and glue together a cheerful pencil top that would encourage someone to write home.

Older people could help younger ones to sew a few stitches in a short 'sleeve' to fit over the end of a pencil. The sleeves can be decorated to look like animals, flowers, fish, insects, vehicles or monsters or they can just be abstract. If the budget allows, you could include the pencil with this craft: supermarkets are doing very good value packs nowadays.

Talk about
During this activity, talk about keeping in touch with people we love—by phone, email, cards, or talking. How does God like us to keep in touch with him?

CELEBRATION

Songs

✛ A-oh, a-ooh let's get funky (4)
✛ Come to the Father (11)
✛ Father God, I wonder (17)

Storytelling

Here's a reflective retelling of the parable of the two sons, slightly adapted from a version by Sue Doggett.

You will need: A green felt underlay, measuring approximately 1 metre square; a piece of felt in a different shade of green to the base cloth, measuring approximately 20cm square; some small wooden trees; a treasure chest containing some chocolate coins; three small wooden figures; a strip of grey felt, measuring approximately 10cm by 80cm; a piece of red felt, measuring approximately 20cm square; a set of toy stacking beakers; a piece of grey felt, measuring approximately 20cm square; some toy (farmyard) pigs; some party poppers or streamers

Lay out a green underlay.

I wonder what this could be?

Place a square of different green-coloured felt in the corner to your right, nearest you. On it, place some small wooden trees and a treasure chest containing chocolate coins. As you say the following words, place the three small figures on the small square in front of the treasure chest.

There was once a farmer who had two sons. One day the younger boy went to his father and said, 'Dad, I can't wait until you die. Give me my share of the farm now!'

How did the farmer feel? We don't know, but he did give the boy his share.

Take the coins out of the chest and divide them into two equal piles. Leave one on the farm and take hold of the other.

Not long after that, the younger boy took his money and left home. He set off to a faraway place.

Roll out a strip of grey felt for a road and spread it out from the farm to the

furthest side from you, in the centre. Move the boy along it. Set up the 'city' by placing a square of red felt at the end of the road and building up a towering cityscape using toy plastic stacking boxes. Move the boy figure into it.

And when he arrived, he had a fantastic time with fantastic friends and spent fantastic amounts of money.

Drop the coins into the cityscape.

But after a while, the money ran out, just at the moment when there was a food shortage in that country. And the boy realized, if he was ever going to eat again, he needed to find a job. But the only job he could find...

Place a grey felt square to your left and put some pigs on it. Move the boy figure to the pigs.

... was looking after pigs. He was so hungry, he would happily have eaten the pigswill, but nobody gave him a thing. But one day he came to his senses and said to himself, 'What am I doing here? Even my father's servants get better treatment than this. I know! I'll go home and say sorry to my dad and maybe he'll let me work for him again.'

And with this decision made, he left the pigs and started out on his long journey home.

Move the boy figure back through the city and to the top of the road. As you say the following words, move the dad figure along the road, then bring them back together to the farm and place some party poppers or streamers on the farm.

But when he was still a long way off, his dad saw him. What would he do? The father ran at full speed down the road towards his son. His son fell to his knees and started his little prepared speech, but his dad picked him up, gave him a big hug and called out, 'Someone get him some clean clothes to wear! Someone get making some food! We've got to party! My son was lost and now he's found! He was dead, but now he's alive!' And all the people on the farm came in and started to celebrate.

Move the older boy figure outside the farm square. As you say the following words, move the father out to him.

All except the older boy, that is. When he discovered what the party was for, he went outside and wouldn't come in. Finally, his father went out to see what the matter was.

'It's not fair!' said the boy. 'All this time I've been working for you and you've never even given me so much as a bag of crisps to enjoy with my friends. But this layabout comes home after wasting all your money and you throw a huge party for him. It's not fair!'

'Oh my son,' said the father. 'You're always with me and everything I have is yours. But don't you see, we had to celebrate, because your brother was lost and now he's found. He was dead and now he's alive.'

Some wondering questions

Ask some wondering questions, such as:

✛ I wonder how the dad felt when his son asked for the money…
✛ I wonder why the dad gave the money to his son…
✛ I wonder how the dad felt when his son went away…
✛ I wonder how the dad got on with the older son…
✛ I wonder why the dad ran down the road towards his younger son…
✛ I wonder how the dad felt about both sons at the end of the story…

Prayer response

When we pray, we're talking to our heavenly Father, who loves us. What would we like to thank our heavenly Father for today? Call out suggestions and say together: 'Thank you, God our Father.'

What would we like to ask God our heavenly Father for today? Hold out two hands open and ask him quietly for: something for someone we love... something for ourselves... Amen

Takeaway menu

✣ Invite everyone to draw, when they get home, their own version of the journey of the boy in the story, adding on lots of colourful detail.

✣ Practise hugging: the challenge is to hug everyone else in the family at least ten times during the day. When this has been achieved, eat doughnuts as a prize. (They're sort of round and huggy.)

✣ Let off a party popper each at a mealtime and, as you let it off, shout out what you love about your family.

✣ Find a safe place, such as a garden or a suitable park, and play hide and seek together.

✣ Each person has done something wonderful today. What is it? Find out and celebrate by having a mini-party with fizzy drink in wine glasses and sausages on sticks, crisps and jelly. Don't forget speeches and toasts.

UNIT 2

Love your neighbour!

This unit is one of a series on love.

AIM

To encourage people to love unconditionally.

BIBLE BACKGROUND (Luke 10:25–37)

The parable of the enemies (The good Samaritan)

This parable is an obvious one to choose, I know, but it is such a great story and has excellent bandits! Furthermore, it is so key to Jesus' whole attitude to outsiders that I make no excuse for using it. What is it that stops the priest and the Levite from helping? Is it their very religion that gets in the way of their being useful in the world? And in what ways is Jesus like the good Samaritan to the world?

FOOD

Bandit food

Sausage and mash with baked beans.

ACTIVITIES

Sandals

You will need: Rubber-coated foam (or floppy plastic tablecloth), PVA glue (or a glue gun), sequins, scissors

Stand a friend on a piece of rubber-coated foam (a find in the craft bank: an alternative might be to use strong but floppy plastic, such as plastic tablecloth material) and trace round their feet, leaving about a centimetre all round. Cut out the shapes. Use PVA glue (or a carefully supervised glue gun) to glue a narrow rectangle of the same material over the width of the shape to make a mule-style sandal. Decorate by gluing on sequins.

Craft banks or scrap stores can be found in certain parts of the UK and are invaluable for a ready supply of interesting card, paper and other items. You can find out if there is one near you by looking at the website www.childrensscrapstore.co.uk, where there is a directory of scrap stores. You could also contact your local Diocesan or Area Children's Advisor to see if they have any sources of craft equipment.

Talk about
During this activity, talk about stepping into other people's shoes or going on a journey.

First aid box

You will need: White cardboard box, felt-tipped pens, fabric sticking plasters

Colour a red cross on a small white cardboard box. Using felt-tipped pens, decorate three or four fabric sticking plasters and put them in your first aid box.

Talk about
During this activity, talk about who helps you when you are hurt. You might also tell the story of the Red Cross and the Red Crescent (do an Internet search on 'history of Red Cross').

Bandit mask or headscarf

You will need: A strip of dark material per person, scissors

Trim the material to fit each person's head, cut eye slits to make a mask, or knot the material around their head in a suitably rakish manner.

Talk about
During this activity, talk about disguises.

Bandit target practice

You will need: Water pistols, plastic bottles

Line up some large plastic bottles as targets for people to blast at with different water pistols. (Avoid any suggestion that the targets are human or it all gets unpleasant.)

Talk about
During this activity, talk about anything really—it's just for fun.

Fence painting

You will need: Tough painter's brushes and buckets of water

Paint an outside fence or wall to look like a mountainous rocky landscape full of caves—a scary place to be!

Talk about
During this activity, talk about desolate landscapes.

Cheese biscuit snack

You will need: Crackers, cheese, raw vegetables

Decorate cheese crackers with squirty cheese from a tube and small pieces of raw vegetable.

Talk about
During this activity, talk about food you might take on journeys.

'Who is my neighbour?' collage

You will need: Collage materials, scissors, PVA glue, felt-tipped pens

Design a collage around hearts and faces of different colours and ages with the title, 'Who is my neighbour?'

Talk about

During this activity, talk about people you know and people you have heard of on the news from other countries.

Flag painting

You will need: Paper, paint, brushes

Paint the national flag of another country that is special to your church or area—a link diocese or twin town, for example—or the birthplace of a member of the team or of one of the people who comes to Messy Church.

Talk about

During this activity, talk about a country special to your church and what the church does to promote the link.

Friendship chain

You will need: Strips of paper, pens, PVA glue (or stapler)

Invite each person to write their name on and decorate at least one strip of paper, which is then stuck in a loop interlinked with others to form a paper chain.

Talk about

During this activity, talk about who your friends are and about people who don't have many friends.

Trinity banner

You will need: An artistic person, craft materials, pictures of world flags, PVA glue

Glue flags from lots of countries on to the section of the banner for 'love your neighbour' (see page 79).

Talk about
During this activity, talk about different countries.

CELEBRATION

Songs

✣ Help me be your eyes (25)
✣ Is there a plank in your eye? (43)
✣ You can reach out (103)

As everyone comes in, show a PowerPoint display of photographs of the session, accompanied by the soundtrack 'He ain't heavy, he's my brother' (The Hollies).

Storytelling

Re-enact the story of the 'good enemy'. Sit everyone along two sides of a nave or central alleyway to make a road. They provide as many sound effects as you ask for (feet walking, owls hooting, wind whistling and so on). Choose people to be the traveller, the bandits, the priest, the temple helper, the man from Samaria and the donkey (you could also have an innkeeper). Ask your 'cast' to act out the story as you tell it in your own words or read it from Luke 10:25–37.

Finish up with the question: what do you do to love people you don't like?

Prayer response

Show a bunch of grapes. Explain that Jesus said we are not like separate grapes; we are like grapes in a bunch—all together with people from other households, other towns, other countries and so on.

Give everyone a grape to hold. Say, 'Before we eat, let's thank God for his love for us. Father God, thank you that you love me.'

Invite everyone to taste their grape. Then pray that everyone may share God's love with their brothers, sisters, mums, dads, school friends and the people they meet every day.

Finish by saying, 'Father God, help me to love all people. Amen'.

Takeaway menu

✤ When you walk to school, to work or to the shops, pray for three people you see on the way. Your prayer might be, 'Dear God, please give this person a really good day today and let them notice you somewhere in it.'

✤ Smile at someone you don't like.

✤ Collect all the loose change in the house and give it to the Samaritans.

✤ Find out if you have any relations in other parts of the world and find where they live on a map.

UNIT 3

Love your world!

This unit is the last in a series on love.

AIM

To nurture a sense of wonder and love for the world God has given us to live in.

BIBLE BACKGROUND (Psalm 8)

The wonderful name of the Lord

So many of us live in urban areas with little chance to be gobsmacked by the size of the starry sky at night, or by the glory of a sunset. Church should be a place where we encourage our members to reconnect with the created world, with all the healing beauty it has to offer and all the lessons we have to learn from it. We need to remember our identity as insignificant dots in the whole history of the universe, who nevertheless are loved to bits by the Creator. We need to remember our responsibility to our planet as we reaffirm our relationship to it. If we can't take Messy Church out into nature, how much nature can we bring into Messy Church?

FOOD

Ploughman's tea

This went down surprisingly well with all, considering how healthy it is.

ACTIVITIES

Pavement artists

You will need: Big sticks of chalk, a paved (or tarmac) outside area

Decorate an outside area of tarmac or concrete with beautiful drawings from the creation story in Genesis 1:1—2:4.

Talk about
During this activity, talk about how today has been for you all.

Sock dragonflies

You will need: Old socks, polyester stuffing, coated wire, tissue paper, googly eyes, PVA glue, string

Stuff a sock and knot the open end. Tie wire wings around the sock's tummy to pinch it in at the waist. Paste tissue paper strips over the wing outlines and stick eyes on the front. Suspend by a string.

Talk about
During this activity, talk about the natural food chains in the beautifully balanced world.

Fish in a jar

You will need: Clean baby food jars and lids or other small lidded jars, baby oil, water, Plasticene, glass paints and paintbrushes (optional)

Make a fish out of Plasticene, small enough to fit in the jar with plenty of room. Half fill the jar with water, add the fish and top up with baby oil. Replace the lid firmly! The fish should float. You could paint on weeds or coral with glass paint.

Talk about
During this activity, talk about the wonder of the seas.

Bird tables

You will need: Pieces of wood about 30cm square, a hand drill, cord

Drill a hole in each corner of the wood, thread through the cord and hang from a branch of a tree.

Talk about
During this activity, talk about birds.

Bowl bugs

You will need: Disposable plastic bowls, pipe cleaners, stickers, sticky tape

Decorate the upturned bowl with stickers to make a spotty bug. Tape the pipe cleaners inside so that they stick out as six legs. Make some eyes from stickers.

Talk about
During this activity, talk about mini-beasts and which one is your favourite.

Vase of daisies

You will need: Small glass bottles, glass paints, somewhere to pick daisies

Decorate the bottle with the paints and fill with daisies.

Talk about
During this activity, talk about the beautiful flowers all round us.

Leaf vein printing

You will need: Leaves with obvious veins, sponges, poster paint, paper

Dab paint on the leaves and print carefully to see the veins.

Talk about

During this activity, talk about the detail in the world.

Marzipan fruits of the earth

You will need: Ready-made marzipan, food colourings, modelling tools, small paintbrushes, petit four cases, pictures of a variety of fruits

Make fruit from marzipan. There are lots of examples to copy online.

NB: Be aware of nut allergies in this activity and, if in doubt, use ready-made icing.

Talk about

During this activity, talk about all the food we get from the natural world.

Creation noticeboard

You will need: Collage materials (card, coloured papers, fabrics and so on), scissors, PVA glue

Design a display with a large planet being held in two even larger hands. People can draw and cut out some of the wonderful animals, plants, birds and fish that live there and stick them on around it.

Talk about

During this activity, talk about organizations that care for the planet.

Trinity banner

You will need: An artistic person, craft and collage materials, and the nearly finished banner from pages 79 and 90

Finish off the banner and display it.

Talk about
During this activity, talk about the three 'loves' you've been working on over these three months (love God, love your neighbour, love your world).

CELEBRATION

Songs

✣ Have we made our God too small? (23)
✣ Lovely jubbly (58)
✣ Nothing's too big (64)
✣ He's got the whole world in his hands (traditional)

Show a PowerPoint display of photographs of the session as everyone comes in.

Storytelling

Start by saying that today we've been thinking about loving the world that God has given us to look after for him. But what a mess we make!

Next, show a short clip of DVD or PowerPoint pictures of exciting things from the natural world (such as starscapes, seas, fluffy creatures, dangerous creatures, ancient trees, tiny details on a butterfly's wing and so on). While you are watching, invite everyone to think of what they like best about God's world. What can we do to look after our planet better?

Once there was a man called David. As a young boy he looked after sheep on hills. He used to pass the time making up songs. When he grew up, he became a great king. Some of his songs became famous: 'The Lord is my shepherd' is one of his songs that a lot of people still sing today.

Here is one of David's songs about God's world. Let's say it together:

O Lord, our God,
Everyone can see how amazing you are!

When I think how huge the sky is,
About the moon and the stars
Which you made and put into place,
I wonder why you care about little people like us!

But you do, and you've given us humans special honour.
You've put us in charge of your whole creation:
Over all the flocks and herds of animals,
Over all the birds in the sky,
Over all the fish and creatures in the sea.

O Lord, our God,
Everyone can see how amazing you are!
PSALM 8 (ADAPTED)

Finish by explaining that our job is to love creation, to care for it, and not to spoil it. Throw an inflated plastic globe from one person to another. Invite whoever catches it to shout out what they like best about God's creation.

Prayer response

Spend a few minutes reflecting on what people might think of doing to help look after God's world. Finish with a simple prayer, such as, 'Dear God, please help us to do all these things. Amen'.

Takeaway menu

✢ Give each person an inexpensive blue plastic ball and the words of Psalm 8 (see above) on an attractive card.
✢ Invite everyone to put the ball somewhere where everyone at home can see it and pray for the world we live in.
✢ Invite everyone to look up at the stars and say David's poem.
✢ Give everyone a printed copy of the story of Jesus calming the storm (Matthew 8:23–27). Invite people to read the story.
✢ Invite people to talk together in the home about one thing they could do this month to help save the world—and do it!

UNIT 4

Christmas

This unit is one in a series about Jesus growing up.

AIM

To overcome the problem that many people see Jesus as a tiny baby one minute and grown up and dying on a cross the next. Also to demonstrate that, in the same way that we do, Jesus went through the process of growing up.

BIBLE BACKGROUND (Luke 2:1–21; Matthew 2:1–12)

Jesus the light for the world

Christmas is a perfect celebration for Messy Church: it demonstrates the way that God himself comes down and graces our ordinary everyday lives with his holy presence, bringing the sacred into the ordinary and hallowing it. God sent Jesus to be cared for—not, like the young Samuel, in a religious community set apart from the world, but in a family. If ever we needed assurance that God thinks families are fantastic, we find it here. What does Mary do? She wraps him in cloths—just as God made clothes for Adam and Eve (Genesis 3:21)—so the roles are reversed and humans care for God by keeping him warmly clothed. God wants to live in the lives of the most ordinary people.

FOOD

Christmas fare

Turkey pie and mash.

ACTIVITIES

Gift of time

> **You will need**: Card, pens, envelopes

Prepare cards with the following wording.

I

....

hereby give you

....

a present of

....

with lots of love

Invite people to decorate the cards and envelopes and fill in the gaps with the appropriate names and a present of 'walking the dog once' or 'vacuuming the lounge in January' or 'painting your toenails' or a similar gift of time and effort that they could give to someone.

Talk about
During this activity, talk about how to show love in different ways. It's often about giving something up for the sake of the other person.

Wise person's hat

You will need: A selection of sticky tape, scissors, card, paper and decorations

Design and make a hat for one of the wise men to wear when they come to see Jesus. A few prototypes can get the creative juices flowing, or some pictures printed off from a search on 'hats' under Google images. You could do a search on 'Design your own hat'.

Talk about
During this activity, talk about the wise men who came to see Jesus when he was young (Matthew 2:1–12).

Angel mobile

You will need: Card, lots of glitter, holographic paper shapes and foil

Make an angel to your own design. Collect the angels and suspend them from a hoop, fairly densely packed but with enough room to move, and hang the finished mobile up in church to enjoy over the Christmas period.

Talk about
During this activity, talk about the angels telling the shepherds about Jesus' birth (Luke 2:8–20).

Nappies

You will need: A life-sized baby doll, terry nappies, disposable nappies, nappy pins, sheeting (optional)

Invite people to learn how to fold and put on a terry nappy with a pin, and how to put on a disposable nappy. If you had some squares of sheeting, people could also put nappies on each other over their clothes, which is fun if all parties are willing.

Talk about
During this activity, talk about Jesus being born as a baby, just like babies are born today.

Graffiti wall

You will need: A huge piece of card or thick paper marked out in brick shapes (you can buy wallpaper with a brick pattern as a more expensive alternative), paint, brushes

Invite everyone to paint Christmas greetings to passers-by on the wall.

Talk about
During this activity, talk about Jesus being born in a very rough place.

Edible baby

You will need: Bun cases, biscuits to fit in them, shredded wheat, icing, jelly baby, fondant icing

Make a manger for the baby by placing a round biscuit in the base of a bun case (you may have to use homemade biscuits to make them small enough). Stick on some shredded wheat cereal with a blob of icing for the hay and make a baby out of a jelly baby swaddled in fondant icing to place on top.

Talk about
During this activity, talk about the good things we have to eat at Christmas time.

Print wrapping paper

You will need: A star-shaped pastry cutter or a circular bottle top, tissue paper, metallic paint

Print a repeated pattern with metallic paint on to bright-coloured tissue paper. When the paper is dry, take it home and use it to wrap a present.

Talk about
During this activity, talk about the fun of giving presents.

Christmas bauble

You will need: Funky art foam or card, scissors, PVA glue, golden glitter, coloured sequins, strong, shiny thread and darning needle

Cut a circle (about 12cm diameter) out of white or golden card or art foam, and then cut out its middle to make a ring. Cut a blue or green circle of card or art foam to fit, freely moving, inside the ring. Cut a candle shape out of the blue or green circle. Glue golden glitter and sequins on to both sides of the outer ring to represent the brightness of heaven. Glue blue and green sequins on to both sides of the inner circle to represent the world. Thread the two pieces together with the world inside the heavens, using a shiny thread, so that the world rotates within the bigger 'heavenly' ring. You could write 'Jesus is the light for the world' on the outside ring. Hang the bauble on a Christmas tree at home.

Talk about
During this activity, talk about Jesus as the light for the world (John 1:4; 8:12).

Christmas noticeboard collage

You will need: Cardboard shapes to wrap, wrapping paper, prepared display, tag shapes, pens, sticky tape

Have the basics of a picture with a baby in a manger in the centre, appearing as if from a Christmas present. Everyone can take a cardboard shape, wrap it in Christmas wrapping paper with streamers and bows, and stick it around the manger. Each person also makes a large gift tag that says 'Happy Christmas to [name] with love from God'. The tags are then stuck on to the manger.

Talk about
During this activity, talk about Jesus being the best present of all.

Junk stable

> **You will need**: Lots of boxes and big containers, other junk, string and sticky tape

Invite everyone to make a stable for Jesus, complete with junk animals, manger and people.

Talk about
During this activity, talk about Jesus' birthplace.

CELEBRATION

Songs

✣ 'Show me the way to shine for Jesus' (Christmas song from the Ideas section on www.barnabasinchurches.org.uk)
✣ Christmas songs known to all

Show a PowerPoint display of photographs of the session as everyone comes in.

Storytelling

Begin by asking everyone if they are looking forward to Christmas. What are they looking forward to most? Perhaps... presents!

I wonder which you like best, getting or giving presents? When I count to three, shout 'We-hey!' if you prefer getting presents and 'Yabadoo!' if you prefer giving presents. I wonder why we give presents at Christmas. It's not everyone's birthday! Perhaps it's to show our love for one another... and perhaps to remind us of the first Christmas present.

The first Christmas present wasn't wrapped in bright shiny paper, but in strips of cloth. The first Christmas present wasn't under the tree or in a stocking: this present was lying in an animals' feeding trough. There was no tag to say who this present was for, but the angel told the shepherds that it was good news for everyone.

This was the first and best Christmas present: baby Jesus, God's Son.

The angels could have shouted 'Yabadoo!' because they knew God loves giving presents, but actually they sang, 'Praise God in heaven! Peace on earth to everyone who pleases God.' When the shepherds saw the baby, they could have shouted 'We-hey!' but in fact they praised God and said wonderful things about him, because of all they had seen and heard.

Christmas is a time to shout, 'We-hey!' We praise God because he gives us so many presents: our life, this wonderful world, our family and those who care for us, our friends, food and fun—and all the things we enjoy at Christmas. To show his love for the world, at Christmas God gave Jesus as a present to everyone. (*Show a picture of the crib with names on it from the craft session*). We-hey!

When someone gives you a present you need to:

✛ Receive it.
✛ Unwrap it.
✛ Say 'thank you'.
✛ Enjoy it.
✛ Share it by showing others.

It's the same with the first and best Christmas present. We need to:

✣ Receive God's present by welcoming Jesus into our homes and our lives.
✣ Unwrap God's present by listening to more of the story of Jesus' life and getting to know him better.
✣ Say 'thank you' for God's present by singing carols to praise and thank him.
✣ Enjoy God's present by treasuring and keeping Jesus as our friend, and by conversing with him in prayer every day.
✣ Share God's present by showing others what a wonderful present Jesus is, and how God loves to give his present to everyone. Yabadoo!

Prayer response

Display the response in bold on a projection screen. Invite people to hold their hands out and close their eyes as if to receive a present.

Leader: Our Father God, we thank you for giving us the gift of Jesus your Son. Help us all to receive him and know him with glad and thankful hearts, and to share your gift of love with everyone. Father God...

All: Thank you for Jesus, your present of love.

Invite everyone to open their eyes and then to place their hands over their eyes so that it is dark.

Leader: Our Father God, we think of all the people in the world for whom this Christmas will be a dark, sad or difficult time. Send them help, send them hope, send them the gift of your love and light. Father God...

All: Thank you for Jesus, your present of love.

Invite everyone to take their hands away from their eyes and reach up high.

Leader: Our Father God, thank you for Christmas. Help us to lift up Jesus with our carols and songs of praise so that everyone can see his glory and join the celebration. Father God…

All: Thank you for Jesus, your present of love.

Takeaway menu

✣ Provide a small present-shaped collecting box and a tealight candle. You could extend the angel-making activity above and invite families to take a bag of materials to give to another family they know, who could make an angel and bring it to church to add on to the mobile at a Christingle or carol service. The other church congregations could also be invited to contribute an angel to make a really spectacular mobile.

✣ Christmas is a time for giving: can you fill the box with money to give away to your favourite charity?

✣ Light the candle together and ask God to shine his light on someone who needs it.

✣ Explain to someone who wasn't at Messy Church what one of your crafts is all about.

UNIT 5

Jesus is found
in the temple

This unit is one in a series about Jesus growing up.

AIM

To see that Jesus was young, and that he grew up to have a faith of his own.

BIBLE BACKGROUND (Luke 2:41–52)

Lost and found

In the story of Jesus in the temple, was Jesus lost? I don't think so! Mary and Joseph certainly lost him—and lost sight of who he was for three days (otherwise they would have looked for him in the temple straight away). There is something in the story about Jesus finding his own identity, but also a warning to parents to give their children space to discover God for themselves. There is also an opportunity to think about the way we can lose sight of Jesus, even though he remains as dear to us as a son to a mother. Just as Aslan, in C.S. Lewis' *Narnia Chronicles*, is not a 'tame lion', Jesus is not a 'tame child'. Jesus is a young man so much in love with God and with his word that he has to be in his Father's house. His love for the temple from this young age makes his later grief over Jerusalem, on his last visit there, even more poignant.

FOOD

Tweeny treats

Bangers, beans and mash

ACTIVITIES

Heart treasure box

You will need: A small heart-shaped box (available from Hobbycraft or other craft outlets), beads, sequins or cut-outs from magazines, PVA glue

Decorate the box. Use it to store a collection of small treasures.

Talk about
During this activity, talk about what Jesus meant when he said, 'Your heart will always be where your treasure is' (Matthew 6:21). Jesus' treasure was God his Father. What do you treasure?

Treasure hunt

You will need: Clues and prizes

Set up a simple picture- or object-based treasure hunt that takes everyone round your entire accessible grounds, with prizes for all who take part.

Talk about
During this activity, talk about looking for treasure and looking for something lost.

Prayer scroll

You will need: Paper, cocktail sticks, beads, calligraphy pen, PVA glue, scissors, thread or thin ribbon (optional)

Cut some parchment-type paper into a strip about 12cm long and 8cm wide. Fold a small amount down at each end and glue a blunted cocktail stick into the fold. Glue a bead on to each of the four ends of the sticks, then roll the scroll up towards the middle from both ends. You could write a question to ask God on the scroll, roll it up and fasten it with a piece of thread or thin ribbon.

Talk about
During this activity, talk about how the books that Jesus read were really scrolls.

Body mural

You will need: A large piece of paper on the floor and different coloured felt-tipped pens or wax crayons

Invite people to lay a body part on the paper and have a friend or family member draw round it. Let the different shapes overlap. Colour in some of the resulting shapes, or fill them with patterns. Look at the different sizes of hands... feet... heads... legs.

Talk about
During this activity, talk about how we grow during our lives.

Growth chart

You will need: A strip of paper with a measure marked on one side (use a published height chart as a guide), pens

Decorate the rest of the height chart with growing things: trees, flowers, animals and so on.

Talk about
During this activity, talk about how Jesus, in the same way that we grow, grew up from being a baby to a small child, a young man and then an adult.

Cress growing

You will need: Cress seeds, paper kitchen towel (or squares of flannel), a planting tray or container such as clean eggshells, or potatoes

Sprinkle cress seeds on paper kitchen towel pads or flannel squares, on potato heads, in eggshells or whatever takes your fancy.

Talk about
During this activity, talk about things that grow.

Heart mint creams

You will need: Peppermint cream mixture, chocolate, sprinkles, glacé icing

Roll out the mixture and cut in to heart shapes. Dip in melted chocolate or stick on sprinkles, if desired, with glacé icing.

Talk about
During this activity, talk about how God loves us all through our lives, whether we are small or big.

Tent making

You will need: Lots of blankets, tablecloths, sheets, chairs, clothes horses and similar

Invite everyone to make dens to sleep in on the way to Jerusalem.

Talk about
During this activity, talk about the way Jesus and his family would go up to Jerusalem for the festivals and would have to camp on the way.

'Mary finds Jesus' collage

You will need: Collage materials

Make a big picture for the noticeboard of the moment when Mary comes and finds Jesus in the temple.

Talk about
During this activity, talk about today's story and how everyone might have felt when Jesus was apparently lost and then found.

Christmas card scenes

You will need: Old Christmas cards, scissors, paper, pens, PVA glue

Cut out a scene from Jesus' birth and stick it on one side of a strip of paper. Then, on the rest of the paper, draw what Jesus might have looked like when he was two and the wise men visited him, and what he might have looked like at whatever age the artist is now (if between two and twelve), and what he might have looked like at twelve years old.

Talk about
During this activity, talk about the twelve years that passed between Jesus being born as a baby in Bethlehem and today's story.

CELEBRATION

Songs

✣ Faith as small as a mustard seed (15)
✣ I would be lost without you (38)

Show a PowerPoint display of photographs of the session as everyone comes in.

Storytelling

Show some photographs of one person from your church as a baby, a toddler, a child, a teenager, then as an adult. Can people guess who it is?

How amazing to think that we all start off as tiny babies, unable to do anything for ourselves. Then very soon we grow up and learn to do many things, such as... *(elicit some answers, such as walking, talking, feeding ourselves and so on)*. Gradually we grow up, and we need bigger... *(elicit some answers, such as shoes and clothes)*. As we grow, we learn new things and make new friends.

It's amazing to think that God's Son was born as a baby just like us! Just like us, Jesus grew up and became a toddler; in the same way that we do, he learned to walk and to talk and to read. Every year, as Jesus grew up, Mary and Joseph would take him with them to Jerusalem for the Passover holiday. Hands up if you usually go on holiday with your family... Where have you been? Everybody used to go to Jerusalem for the annual Passover celebration of God's love. The temple was the focus of the celebration, which was like a six-week-long party. It took several days to walk from Nazareth, and several days to walk back (some of you made tents to live in on the way), but, with families and friends travelling together, a good time was had by all... until the year Jesus was twelve.

Is anyone here twelve this month? That's how old Jesus was when Mary and Joseph lost Jesus! It was on the way back from Jerusalem that they noticed he was missing. Their first thought was that Jesus must be walking with other friends and relations in the crowd, but after a whole day travelling without seeing Jesus, they began to wonder where he was. They looked for him among family and friends and asked everyone if they had seen Jesus—but the answer was always 'No'.

Jesus was missing! By now, Mary and Joseph were very worried. They hurried back to Jerusalem to look for him. They searched everywhere: in the house where they had stayed, in the streets, in the market. They asked everyone if they had seen Jesus—but the answer was always 'No'.

Finally they found him! Guess where? They found him in the temple, listening to the teachers and asking questions. How do you think Mary and Joseph felt? 'Why have you done this to us?' they asked him. Jesus said something that surprised them and stuck in their minds from that day forward. He said, 'Why did you need to look for me? Didn't you know I would be in my Father's house?'

Mary and Joseph didn't understand what Jesus meant, but perhaps they realized that Jesus was really growing up—because he was asking questions about God and wanting to be closer to his heavenly Father.

Mary kept on thinking about all that had happened. It is good for us, too, to treasure this story and remember that, like us, Jesus grew up. Whatever age we are, God our heavenly Father wants us, like Jesus, to ask our questions and grow up to know him better.

Finish with the song, 'Father we adore you', sung as a round with actions.

Father we adore you (slowly spread hands from the centre)
Lay our lives before you (bring hands together and move them forward in the sign of an offering)
How we love you (gather hands to heart)

Prayer response

Read out some questions from the scrolls you have made. Ask what things we need to thank God for. Finish each question or thanksgiving with the words 'Father, we thank you'.

Next, invite everyone to think of someone who needs God's love and help... to picture that person in their minds... and to imagine them being touched by Jesus. Finish with the words, 'Father, please hear our prayers. Amen'.

Takeaway menu

✣ Make a map of the streets around your home, with important places drawn in.

✣ Say a prayer for people who are lost and lonely, especially if they have lost their family.

✣ Go into your local church and spend a few moments quietly inside.

✣ Go to someone you think is wise and ask them the hardest question you can think of about God.

UNIT 6

Lent

This unit is one in a series about Jesus growing up.

AIM

To learn about the time when Jesus was grown up and decided it was time to begin his work.

BIBLE BACKGROUND (Luke 4:1–13)

Jesus and the devil

Growing up is all about coming to maturity, to an 'owned faith' that stands up to anything that is thrown at it. It is about knowing who we are in God's eyes, with such certainty that we don't need to take any short cuts or settle for second best. In the story of Jesus and the devil, the maturity of Jesus' faith was sorely tested. This story also reminds us of the importance of continuing to make ourselves familiar with God's word, so that it is to hand when we need it most.

FOOD

Bean feast

Jacket potatoes, cheese, beans, French bread.

ACTIVITIES

Lent journey

You will need: Strips of paper, pens, stickers

Christians often compare life to a journey. On a long strip of paper, draw a road that goes through lots of different sorts of landscapes—some pretty and sunny, some boggy and dangerous. Some suggestions might be mountains, caves, seaside, woods, jungle, volcanoes, cities, villages, marsh, desert, ice and so on. This Lent, take 40 stickers home with you and, every day, stick a sticker on the sort of landscape that the day has felt like to you. For example, on difficult days, you might stick the sticker on a mountain or in a cave; on exciting days, it might be like the seaside, and so on. Pray for the other people in your family as you find out where their sticker goes.

Talk about
During this activity, talk about what Christians do during Lent.

Cross to wear

You will need: Thick tin foil (such as the foil of a pie dish), scissors, pencil

Carefully cut a small cross out of the foil, then use a pencil to 'emboss' patterns on it, such as dots (for the nails) or teardrop shapes (for the tears of the women) or circles (for God's unending love) or short lines (for the thorns). *A-cross the World* by Martyn Payne and Betty Pedley (Barnabas, 2004) includes interesting crosses whose patterns might inspire you (especially the aborigine cross).

Talk about

During this activity, talk about why we sometimes wear crosses.

Chocolate parcel

You will need: Chocolate, decorative wrappings, label

Wrap up some chocolate in an attractive parcel with ribbon, bows and so on, and label it with the date of Easter Day. Encourage people to put it somewhere safe and to save it until Easter, when the whole family can take out their chocolate and enjoy it together.

Talk about

During this activity, talk about things that we are prepared to wait patiently for. Sometimes we need to practise with little things so that we can be in training for waiting for bigger things. Lent is a good time to practise.

Easter invitation to Messy Church

You will need: Some invitation cards, pens

Decorate and personalize the invitations (perhaps for the next Messy Church or for another Easter event or service). You could offer to send the invitations by post, if people know the address, or they could deliver them personally.

Talk about

During this activity, talk about how the first disciples went out and told everyone that Jesus had risen from the dead. We can tell people, too, by inviting them to come to Messy Church and hear the story for themselves.

Parachuting person

You will need: Clothes pegs, Plasticene, string, strong paper bags

Weight a clothes peg with some Plasticene and attach a parachute made from a paper bag with string tied on to the corners. Take the peg-person up to the highest point you can, throw it down and see if it floats or drops (on-the-job adjustments may be necessary). This activity keeps older children occupied for a surprising length of time.

Talk about
During this activity, talk about the temptations of Jesus, including the one to jump off the top of the temple. (Jesus refused to jump, but we're going to make a person who does...)

Plaited bread

You will need: Bread dough (see recipe on page 71)

Make a small plaited loaf or roll of bread. If there isn't time to allow it to rise, scone dough could be used instead. The three strands of the plait could be reminders of the three temptations.

Talk about
During this activity, talk about the temptation Jesus had to turn stones into bread.

Bread Bible

You will need: Sliced white bread, thin paintbrushes or cocktail sticks and natural food colourings

Either paint the bread so that it looks like the cover of a Bible, or paint on a short verse, such as Jesus' words, 'I am the bread that gives life!' (John 6:35).

Talk about

During this activity, talk about how Jesus knew the scriptures so well that he could use the words like a sword to fight off the devil. Even when he was really hungry and was thinking about bread, he still knew that people don't live just on food, but also need God's word.

Sand bottle or tray

You will need: Bottle, cooking salt, powder paint, sand tray

Older people might like to fill a bottle with layers of multicoloured 'sand' (cooking salt with powder paint mixed in), and younger people might just like to play in the sand tray.

Talk about

During this activity, talk about the sandy desert where Jesus went to be alone with God.

'Treasures of the world' mural

You will need: A prepared display board, collage materials

Decorate the display board with a picture of the world in the centre and pictures of treasures round the outside of it, perhaps on 'thought bubble' frames or backgrounds. The title could be: 'Does any treasure stop you being close to God?'

Talk about
During this activity, talk about why the devil tested Jesus by showing him all the nations on earth (the world and all its treasures). What was he offering to Jesus? Which treasure would you find it hardest to say 'no' to?

DIY obstacle course

You will need: Sturdy furniture, sheets or blankets, hoops, boxes—in fact, anything you have to hand

Invite everyone to make an obstacle course. Naturally, you will then need to find someone to race through it.

Talk about
During this activity, talk about how hard it can be to live life as a Christian. Sometimes there are things that get in our way and slow us down, but we know that Jesus is always with us and that he knows how frustrating life can be because he went through the same sort of things as we do.

CELEBRATION

Songs

✧ Hands, hands, fingers, thumbs (21)
✧ I will be yours (36)
✧ We are marching in the light of God

Show a PowerPoint display of photographs of the session as everyone comes in.

Storytelling

Talk about reality television shows, such as *Big Brother*. Make the observation that such shows are designed as a test to see what people are really like.

Say: Today's story is like a Bible version of *Big Brother*. It is not set in a house, but in the desert, which is very hot during the day and very cold at night. The desert is dry, dusty and scary. God sent Jesus there all alone for 40 days and, at the end of that time, the devil gave Jesus three tests.

Test 1

Show a stone. Ask people to imagine what it is like to be really hungry, then to imagine how Jesus must have felt. The devil told him to turn stones into bread rolls. But Jesus refused to be tempted, telling the devil that doing what God wants is more important than having food.

Hooray! Jesus has passed the first test. (*Do a thumbs up, or a Mexican wave.*)

Test 2

Show a globe. The devil took Jesus up a high mountain from where it seemed as if he could see the whole world. The devil told Jesus that, if he was God's Son, he surely should be king over the whole world. The devil tried to tempt Jesus by telling him that if Jesus worshipped him, he would make Jesus king of the world with all its treasures. But Jesus refused to be tempted, telling the devil that the scriptures say we should worship the Lord our God and serve only him.

Hooray! Jesus has passed the second test. (Do a thumbs up, or a Mexican wave.)

Test 3

The devil took Jesus to the highest temple tower in Jerusalem and told him that, if he really was God's Son, he could jump off the tower and God would send his angels to catch him. Then everyone would believe in him. But Jesus refused to be tempted, telling the devil that the scriptures say we mustn't try to test God.

Hooray! Jesus has passed the third test. (Do a thumbs up, or a Mexican wave.)

Then the devil left Jesus. The three tests show what Jesus is really like: he is unable to be persuaded to do wrong and he really is God's Son. Jesus really can help us when we face tests in our own lives.

Prayer response

Take the stone. Invite people to pray for those who are hungry. Take the globe. Invite people to pray for world leaders to make wise decisions. Take a cross. Invite people to say 'thank you' to Jesus for undergoing the tests in the desert for us. End with the words, 'Father, hear our prayer. Amen'.

Takeaway menu

✣ *Play and Praise through Lent*, edited by Kay Warrington (Barnabas, 2005), has some fantastic ideas for encouraging families to live Lent together.

✣ The *Live Life, Love Lent* booklets from Church House Publishing are also great.

✣ The Barnabas website has many ideas for Lent.

✣ Send 40 stickers home per person to help them pray with each other on their Lent journey (see 'Lent journey' activity on p. 120).

✣ Throw a pancake party for another family from Messy Church.

✣ Read a little bit of the run-up to Easter every day from a Bible or Bible story book.

✣ Paint stones.

UNIT 7

Spring festivals

This unit is one in a series about Jesus growing up.

AIM

To cover some of the spring festivals, such as Mothering Sunday and Good Friday, and to follow the story of the end of Jesus' life and the new beginning of Easter.

BIBLE BACKGROUND (John 19:16—20:10)

The Easter narratives

In this Messy Church session, we focus on the very centre of the Christian faith, with the stories of Good Friday and Easter Day. For some people, Messy Church might be the only place where they hear the Easter story and begin to understand that Easter is about so much more than chocolate and bunnies. This session ties in with the previous three themes of Christmas, 'Jesus is found in the temple' and Lent, in which we learnt about Jesus' birth, his early years and his growing up to start his work. It is the culmination of the story about why Jesus came into the world.

FOOD

Pitta pockets

Make up a basic mince-based sauce and fill a pitta bread pocket with it. Serve with cucumber or carrot sticks.

ACTIVITIES

Festival cards

You will need: Card-making materials

Find someone who is a card maker and can help everyone design and make beautiful cards for Mothering Sunday or Easter.

Talk about
During this activity, talk about the people who have looked after us as we have grown up.

Paper flowers

You will need: Tissue paper, sticky tape, pipe cleaners

Make multicoloured flowers out of different-sized circles of tissue paper gathered together in the centre. Attach them to a pipe cleaner stalk with sticky tape, which can also be wound around the squished-together part of the petals.

Talk about
During this activity, talk about the way you have to bury a seed to make it grow into a plant that can give you flowers.

Photo frame

You will need: Card, decorations, string, metallic paint

Make a photo frame out of sturdy card decorated with blue flowers to stand for forget-me-nots, or chunky knotted string glued on and painted with a touch of metallic paint, to be like a knot in a hanky for remembering to do something. Put a fold of card on the back to make the frame stand up, or add a loop of string to hang it up by. If you have the facilities, print a picture of someone in the maker's family or friendship group for the centre and stick it in. If not, invite people to stick in a picture at home of the person they'd like to remember.

Talk about
During this activity, talk about remembering all the good things about the people who look after us, and remembering to tell them. Jesus asked his friends to remember him always.

Red nose cakes

You will need: Buns, icing, decorations

Red Nose Day in the UK (Comic Relief) raises money for a variety of charities. Make a red-nosed bun to remind yourself to keep giving out in return for all the good things we have been given. You might also like to make a batch to sell at the next Red Nose Day to raise money for charity. Decorate a basic bun with white icing, two chocolate drops for eyes and anything edible, round and red for a nose, such as a cherry, a sweet or a piece of fruit.

Talk about
During this activity, talk about why we give money to charities.

Big web

You will need: Vast amounts of string or wool

Create a huge web stretched out between chair backs and table legs. Older children and adults can make the web and younger ones can enjoy climbing through it and under it.

Talk about

During this activity, talk about the way Jesus' love ties us all together, linking us into one huge family.

Wotsit flowers

You will need: Multicoloured packing foam chips (the ones that look like Wotsit snacks), water, PVA glue and card (optional)

Moisten the foam chips and stick them together in any form you like. They make rather splendid small flowers, which can then be glued on to a card, if desired.

Talk about

During this activity, talk about springtime and new birth.

Fondant egg nest

You will need: Shredded wheat and chocolate (or sweet shoelaces), fondant icing, food colouring

Make a nest out of either shredded wheat mixed with melted chocolate, or sweet shoelaces cut into short lengths and stuck together into a looped nest shape with icing or melted chocolate. Make some eggs out of fondant icing and paint them with food colouring. Place the eggs in the nest.

Talk about

During this activity, talk about why we use eggs as a symbol at Easter time (to symbolize the rock in front of Jesus' tomb, and new life coming out of something that looks as inanimate as a stone).

Fairtrade chocolate story

You will need: Information about Fairtrade chocolate, collage materials

Make a display showing the route chocolate takes to get to our eggs. You might find a book with the information in it or you could download it from a Fairtrade website. Try to bring the chocolate producers to life and introduce the idea that they can have a better life for themselves and their children if they get a fair price for the chocolate beans they grow.

Talk about

During this activity, talk about chocolate eggs and where chocolate comes from.

International cross-making

> **You will need**: Cross-making equipment as described in
> *A-cross the World* by Martyn Payne and Betty Bedley
> (Barnabas, 2004). This is available as PDF download from
> www.brfonline.org.uk/downloads.

Have a selection of crosses from around the world to make. There are
great ideas in *A-cross the World*, or you could do some searches on the
Barnabas and other websites.

Talk about
During this activity, talk about Jesus choosing to go to the cross for
our sake because he loves us.

Paint an Easter picture

> **You will need**: Paints, brushes and big sheets of paper

Invite people to paint the part of the Easter story that is most
precious to them.

Talk about
During this activity, talk about the Easter story.

CELEBRATION

Songs

✣ Blessed be the name of the Lord (7)
✣ Hands, hands, fingers, thumbs (21)

Show a PowerPoint display of photographs of the session as everyone comes in.

Storytelling

Show a drawing of a large letter 'X'. Say: I used to get a lot of these in Maths because I wasn't very good at sums. What does it mean when you see the letter 'X' after a sum? It means you got it wrong!

But I also got a lot of these on letters from my granny. What does it mean when you see the letter 'X' at the end of a letter? It means lots of kisses—'I love you!'

When Jesus was grown up, about 33 years old (is anyone here 33?), he died on a cross. Jesus' cross is a different shape from these crosses, but it means both these things. It means we got it wrong: Jesus died so that God could forgive us everything we got wrong. But Jesus also died because he loves us so much. Let's hear the story of that sad Friday and that amazing Sunday.

Tell the story using pictures, either by using a children's picture book version of the story of Good Friday and Easter, or by displaying a series of pictures on PowerPoint or something similar. Include the following events. Ideally, tell the story by heart, using the pictures as a guide.

✣ The last supper
✣ Jesus on trial
✣ The three crosses
✣ The tomb with a rock rolled in front of it
✣ The tomb with the rock rolled away
✣ Jesus' friends meeting him after his resurrection

Say: And that is what we remember every Good Friday and Easter Day—that Jesus died for us and that he came back to life so that he can always be with us.

Prayer response

Hold up the letter 'X' again.

Leader: Let's say 'sorry' to God for the things we've got wrong...
All: Sorry, Lord!
Leader: Let's say 'thank you' to God for loving us so much...
All: Thank you, Lord!

Hold up a cross.

Leader: Lord, please help us to share your love with others this Easter time.
All: Amen!

Takeaway menu

✢ Take two wrapped fairly traded chocolate bars or eggs. Eat one and think about the loveliness of Easter Day. Give the other one away to someone who needs some love.
✢ Plant a seed together.
✢ Buy a hot cross bun and talk about why it has a cross on top.
✢ Read the Easter story from a book with good-quality pictures (look in the library or a Christian bookshop).
✢ Invite someone round for an Easter meal and all help with the cooking, decorating the table and serving.

UNIT 8

The story of Ruth

This session is the first of three on the theme of women who lived their lives for God.

AIM

To tell the story of Ruth and to celebrate the festival of harvest.

BIBLE BACKGROUND (Ruth 1:1—4:22)

The book of Ruth

It is good to spend time on three key women in the Old Testament, as Bible heroes tend to be men rather than women. In fact, if you did these three sessions in the lead-up to Christmas, a nice link would be to Mary as a fourth woman who made a difference.

In the book of Ruth, Ruth's love and loyalty to Naomi are celebrated and, although Ruth was an adult, love and loyalty are qualities that even the smallest child can appreciate and value. With its glorious setting in the fields outside Bethlehem, the story is an evocative one for the festival of harvest.

FOOD

Harvest feast

Serve French bread pizza as per the instructions on page 69. As an extra serving suggestion, provide some bread or garlic bread to accompany the meal.

ACTIVITIES

NB: If desired, you could use some of the bread-based activities from other sessions, such as bread making, painting on bread and so on (see index on page 211 for specific activities).

Grinding wheat

You will need: Ears of wheat, pestle and mortar

Provide ears of wheat and invite people to turn them into flour using a pestle and mortar.

Talk about
During this activity, talk about traditional harvest jobs, such as milling.

Gleaning

You will need: Snacks, hay, wrapping paper, sticky tape

Wrap up lots of carrot sticks, celery sticks, stick-shaped crisps, Twiglets and so on in clingfilm or foil. Hide them inside a big trough of hay or straw and invite people to find as many as they can in a 'lucky dip' plunge of their arm. Watch out for people who get hay fever or asthma: you could replace the hay with shredded paper, but you won't get the good smell.

Talk about
During this activity, talk about the ancient practice of rich landowners allowing poor people to glean corn from their fields after the harvesters had gone by.

Harvest picture

You will need: Sugar paper, black marker pen, items such as beans, peas, lentils, shredded tissue paper, pasta shapes and so on, PVA glue

On a large sheet of sugar paper, using a black marker pen, mark out a landscape of hills and fields. Invite people to cover each field in turn with glue and fill it with one of the items suggested above. Try to get as many different textures as possible.

Talk about
During this activity, talk about where bread comes from.

Boaz's blanket

You will need: Blanket, sewing kit, material scraps

Decorate a small blanket either by learning to do blanket stitch round the edge or by choosing a patch of brightly coloured fabric and sewing it on. (Some people may never have held a needle before, so it doesn't matter if they do it roughly.) For older people, you could have a beginners' patchwork quilt session running alongside and, for very young ones, a few shoeboxes, cloths, dolls or teddies will give them the chance to 'put Boaz to bed'.

Talk about
During this activity, talk about Boaz sheltering Ruth kindly under his blanket.

Weaving

You will need: Paper, scissors, ruler, pencils, PVA glue

Draw a border a few centimetres inside the edge of a sheet of paper. Fold the paper in half widthways and cut irregular slits, staying inside the border, so that when you open up the paper, there are slits running nearly the full length of the paper, parallel to the long sides. Weave different coloured strips of paper crossways into this framework, gluing down the ends as you go along.

Talk about
During this activity, talk about weaving as an image for people's lives being woven together, and for the way God's story weaves into ours.

Flour and water paste

You will need: Flour, water, card (optional), salt (optional), clean sticks, a fire

Mix up some flour and water paste to a thick consistency. You can simply show how it can be used as glue, or you could have a competition to see who can stretch out the longest 'string' of paste across a sheet of card. You can also put your whole hand in the paste and see who can make the most interesting temporary sculpture as you raise your hand slowly out of the goo.

If you have access to a campfire or barbecue, you can make paste twirls to eat: add a bit of salt to the paste and wrap it round a clean stick. Standing at a safe distance, turn the twirl over the glowing coals of a barbecue or campfire until it cooks (about ten minutes). Being careful not to burn yourself (well, you will get burnt, but that's part of the fun), break open the twirl, put butter on the inside and eat as much as is edible.

Talk about
During this activity, talk about what we use flour for.

'I believe' handprints

You will need: Paint, paper

On a large sheet of paper, write in large letters, 'I believe in God'. Invite anyone who wants to make a sign of their loyalty to God to paint their hand and make a print of it on the paper.

Talk about
During this activity, talk about the way the story of Ruth reminds us to stay loyal and loving to God.

Dolly peg characters

You will need: 'Dolly' type clothes pegs, scraps of material and PVA glue or sewing kit

Invite people to dress a dolly peg as Ruth, Naomi or Boaz with scraps of material.

Talk about
During this activity, talk about the different people in the story.

Pencil top friends

You will need: Pipe cleaners, funky art foam, 3D glaze pens, googly eyes, PVA glue, pencils

You could make a pencil top as a present for your best friend (or your mother-in-law!). Cut a friendly face out of art foam and add googly eyes and wool strands. Decorate with 3D glaze pens and glue the finished pencil top on to a pipe cleaner. To complete your pencil top friend, wind the pipe cleaner round a pencil.

Talk about
During this activity, talk about who are your friends.

Straw pipes

You will need: Drinking straws (preferably made out of paper), scissors

Paper straws work best, but plastic ones may have to do. Flatten one end of the straw and trim off a diagonal at each side of the flattened part to make a mouthpiece. Blow gently through the mouthpiece and adjust it until it makes a good sound. Make a set of different length straw pipes and see how the note varies in pitch.

Talk about
During this activity, talk about straws we drink from and straw that grows in a field.

CELEBRATION

Songs

✤ Do not fear (13)
✤ Higher higher (28)
✤ I'm gonna jump up and down (40)

Show a PowerPoint display of photographs of the session as everyone comes in.

Storytelling

When things go wrong, we all need someone to help us—someone who cares for us, someone we can rely on, someone loving and loyal.

Ruth was someone like that for Naomi. Naomi's husband and her two sons had died and she was left with no one to care for her. Ruth had been married to one of Naomi's sons, so she, too, was on her own. Naomi told Ruth that it was time to say goodbye. 'You must go back home to your own family and I must go back to where I was born, far away in Bethlehem,' she said.

But Ruth said, 'No! Wherever you go, I'll go. Your people will be my people and your God will be my God.' Naomi was so thankful for Ruth's affection. She had Ruth to rely on—someone loving and loyal.

Together, Naomi and Ruth journeyed back to Naomi's home town of Bethlehem. They arrived just as the barley harvest was beginning. They had no money, so Ruth went out into the fields to glean—that is, to collect the ears of barley that the harvesters had dropped. Ruth worked hard all day, gleaning the grain. She got hot and thirsty and her back ached.

The owner of the field was a man called Boaz. He had heard how loving and loyal Ruth had been to Naomi and, when he saw Ruth gleaning in his field, he said to her, 'May God bless you for your kindness. Help yourself to a drink from the workers' water jars whenever you are thirsty.' Boaz gave Ruth some food, and even told his workers to leave plenty of extra ears of barley for her to gather.

When Ruth got home, she told Naomi about how kind Boaz had been. Naomi smiled for the first time in months. 'That man is our closest relative!' she said. Naomi thought that Boaz would make a good husband for Ruth. He was someone she could rely on—someone loving and loyal.

And, to cut a long story short, Boaz did marry Ruth. Before long, they had a baby boy—much to Naomi's joy and delight. Ruth's baby was called Obed. He became the grandfather of a great king called David. And King David was the great-great-great-(lots of times great) grandfather of the greatest king of all, who was also born in Bethlehem.

His name was... Jesus.

At harvest time we thank God for giving us the food we need. God is someone we can all rely on. He was loving and loyal to Ruth, Naomi and Boaz. He made them part of his great plan to send his Son, Jesus, to be our king and friend—someone we can rely on, someone who is loving and loyal.

Prayer response

Thanks!

Invite everyone to call out at the same time who they are thankful for because of that person's love for them.

All: Lord, thank you for the love and loyalty of...

Please!

Invite everyone to call out at the same time the name of a country where, just as Ruth and Naomi were, there are people who are refugees far from home. Form a prayer asking God to look after them.

All: Lord, please look after the refugees in...

Takeaway menu

✛ Provide a bulb or a few seeds in an envelope. Plant your bulb and wait for it to grow.
✛ Pray your way round the supermarket and thank God for the people who grew each item of food you buy.
✛ When you start a new loaf of bread, trace a cross over it as a sign of God's blessing.
✛ Invite friends for a picnic or barbecue to celebrate harvest time.
✛ Find out what your church is collecting for their harvest festival service and bring some along as an offering to God.

UNIT 9

The story of Hannah

This session is the second of three on the theme of women who lived their lives for God.

AIM

To learn to pray as Hannah prayed.

BIBLE BACKGROUND (1 Samuel 1:1–28)

Hannah asks the Lord for a child

With childlike simplicity, Hannah was open about her grief when she was in the safe space of the temple at Shiloh. Church, too, should be a safe space where grief, questioning and a sense of frustration are welcomed and honoured, rather than frowned upon. From a pastoral point of view, Eli the priest misread the situation in the first instance. How reassuring, though, that God still worked his blessing despite Eli's critical lack of sensitivity! Our God is a God of second chances.

NB: With the story of Hannah, be aware of the need for sensitivity, as there may be women present who, like Hannah, are unable to have children.

145

FOOD

Sausage casserole

Make the casserole using the recipe on page 69. Serve with mash and tinned sweetcorn.

ACTIVITIES

Mosaic notebook cover

You will need: Notebooks, coloured paper, scissors, PVA glue, simple geometric templates

Cut a piece of coloured paper the same size as the notebook cover and glue it on. Copy a simple shape from the templates on to the coloured paper. Cut small squares from further pieces of coloured paper and glue them into the shape in a mosaic pattern.

Talk about
During this activity, talk about the way some Christians keep a note of their prayers in a journal so that they can see how God answers the prayers.

Prayer candle holder

You will need: Tealight candle holder, glitter glue, tealight candles

Decorate a tealight candle holder (or a jar or glass) with glitter glue.

Talk about
During this activity, talk about using candles in prayer.

Prayer hand

You will need: Paper, felt-tipped pens

Draw round your hand and write on each finger as follows.

✣ Thumb: people nearest me
✣ Index finger: people I see around me at school or work
✣ Third finger: important people
✣ Ring finger: people who are unwell
✣ Little finger: me

Decorate the rest of the hand with beautiful or weird designs.

Talk about
During this activity, talk about how to use the prayer hand. Make the comment that we can use our fingers to help us remember who to pray for.

Dead-of-night experience

You will need: Blankets, sheets, masking tape, boxes and so on

Provide blankets and boxes, chairs, tables and masking tape and challenge everyone to create a totally dark route to walk or crawl through.

Talk about
During this activity, talk about the time when Hannah's son, Samuel, was a little boy and heard God calling him at night in the temple. He would have had to walk through the temple all on his own in the dark.

Phone line

You will need: String, clean tin cans, skewer

Using the skewer, punch a hole in the bottom of each tin can. (**NB:** Ensure that adult help is available for younger children.) Make a phone line with a long piece of string stretched between two tin cans, attached through the holes. See how far away from each other you can get and still hear your partner.

Talk about
During this activity, talk about prayer being simply talking to God, very much in the way that people chat on a telephone.

Blessings box

You will need: Matchboxes or similar small boxes, decorations, blessings written out on strips of paper

Decorate the box on the outside to your own taste. You could include the letters BB for 'blessings box'. From the blessings below, choose five that you like and put them in your box, folded or rolled very small. Give out your blessings to different people during the next week.

Blessings

✣ I pray that the Lord will bless and protect you. (Numbers 6:24)

✣ Discover for yourself that the Lord is kind. Come to him for protection and you will be glad. (Psalm 34:8)

✣ You, Lord God, bless everyone who cares for the poor, and you rescue those people in times of trouble. (Psalm 41:1)

✣ Our God, be kind and bless us! Be pleased and smile. (Psalm 67:1)

✣ You bless all who depend on you for their strength and all who deeply desire to visit your temple. (Psalm 84:5)

✣ Lord God All-Powerful, you bless everyone who trusts you. (Psalm 84:12)

✣ Our Lord, you bless those who join in the festival and walk in the brightness of your presence. (Psalm 89:15)

✣ You bless those people who are honest and fair in everything they do. (Psalm 106:3)

✣ May the Lord who created the heavens and the earth give you his blessing. (Psalm 115:15)

✣ God bless the one who comes in the name of the Lord! We praise you from here in the house of the Lord. (Psalm 118:26)

✣ You bless all those who follow your commands from deep in their hearts and who never do wrong or turn from you. (Psalm 119:2–3)

✣ Your fields will produce, and you will be happy and all will go well. (Psalm 128:2)

✣ The Lord is the Creator of heaven and earth, and I pray that the Lord will bless you from Zion. (Psalm 134:3)

✣ The Lord God of Jacob blesses everyone who trusts him and depends on him. (Psalm 146:5)

✣ The Lord blesses everyone who freely gives food to the poor. (Proverbs 22:9)

✣ I will bless those who trust me. (Jeremiah 17:7)

✣ God blesses those people who depend only on him. They belong to the kingdom of heaven! (Matthew 5:3)

✣ God blesses those people who grieve. They will find comfort! (Matthew 5:4)

✤ God blesses those people who are humble. The earth will belong to them! (Matthew 5:5)
✤ God blesses those people who want to obey him more than to eat or drink. They will be given what they want! (Matthew 5:6)
✤ God blesses those people who are merciful. They will be treated with mercy! (Matthew 5:7)
✤ God blesses those people whose hearts are pure. They will see him! (Matthew 5:8)
✤ God blesses those people who make peace. They will be called his children! (Matthew 5:9)
✤ God blesses those people who are treated badly for doing right. They belong to the kingdom of heaven. (Matthew 5:10)
✤ God will bless you when people insult you, ill-treat you, and tell all kinds of evil lies about you because of me. (Matthew 5:11)

Talk about
During this activity, talk about how blessing someone means asking God to do good things for them.

Tuck box

You will need: Ice cream wafer 'oyster shells', sweets, tiny biscuits, grapes, sultanas and so on, natural food colouring, paintbrushes

Paint your name on top of your oyster shell tuck box. Fill it with ten good things to eat.

Talk about
During this activity, talk about how Hannah brought Samuel clothes as he grew up. She might also have brought him treats to eat.

T-shirt decorating

You will need: Pencils, paper, fabric pens, T-shirts, stencils

Draw a design on paper, then decorate a T-shirt.

Talk about
During this activity, talk about how quickly children grow out of clothes.

Get real!

You will need: Circles of different coloured paper, pens, a prepared noticeboard, PVA glue

Decorate the noticeboard with the words, 'Whatever your mood… get real with God!' Invite people to draw a face on a circle that shows a mood they have experienced recently. You might want to print out some emotions as examples. Stick the faces round the words.

Talk about
During this activity, talk about different emotions.

Paint-a-mood

You will need: A huge sheet of paper on the floor, paints and brushes, a list of moods, such as joyful, frightened, worried, triumphant, depressed, distressed, lonely and so on.

Invite people to express the different moods on the paper in colours and patterns or shapes. For added interest, have a concordance to hand so that people can find the moods in the Psalms.

Talk about

During this activity, talk about the different moods we experience.

CELEBRATION

Songs

✢ 24–7 (1)
✢ Any kind of weather (2)
✢ Jump up (48)

Show a PowerPoint display of photographs of the session as everyone comes in.

Storytelling

Begin by asking how many people have made something to do with prayer today. Do we pray only when we are in church? Or only when we are happy? Or only when we are pleased with what God is doing in our lives?

Make the comment that some people try to pretend to God that everything is all right. But God likes it when we are real with him and tell him just what is going on in our lives, whether it is good, bad or terrible. Then he can really help us.

Explain that the story today took place a long time before Jesus was born. It is about a person called Hannah. (Ask if there is anyone present with the name 'Hannah'.)

Hannah couldn't have a baby. Her husband had another wife, which was quite normal in those days, and the other wife had children, but

Hannah had none. The other wife made fun of Hannah. She teased her and made her very miserable. So one day, when the whole family was visiting the temple of God in Shiloh, Hannah went away by herself to pray.

Was she happy? No! Was she calm? No! Was she pleased with the way her life was turning out? No! Did she pretend to God that everything was OK? No! Hannah was sad, bitter and broken-hearted. But, instead of pretending everything was OK, she told God just how she felt.

Perhaps there are some people here today who are sad, angry or fed up with life. Let's be real and tell God about those things now. Hannah knew that when we are real with God, he hears us. She prayed right from her heart and asked God for a son. She promised that if God gave her a son, she would give her son back to God.

Now Eli the priest was sitting in a chair by the door. Although he couldn't hear a word Hannah was saying, he could see her weeping and rocking backwards and forwards. He told her off for being drunk! Poor Hannah! But Hannah didn't go off in a huff. Instead, she told Eli how sad she was and how she had been pouring out her soul to God. So Eli the priest blessed her and asked God to give her what she was asking for.

And, do you know, in time Hannah did have a son—and she knew just what to call him. She was so sure that God had heard her prayers that she called her son Samuel, which means 'God hears'.

Sometimes God answers our prayers in the way we are expecting; sometimes he answers them in a way we aren't expecting, and sometimes he makes us wait and wait and wait for an answer. But he has promised us that he hears our prayers. In Psalm 145 we read the words:

Our Lord, everything you do is kind and thoughtful, and you are near to everyone whose prayers are sincere. You satisfy the desires of all your worshippers, and you come to save them when they ask for help.

PSALM 145:17–19

Prayer response

In our prayers today, let us say together part of the prayer that Hannah said after Samuel was born.

You make me strong and happy, Lord. You rescued me... No other god is like you. We're safer with you than on a high mountain.
1 SAMUEL 2:1–2

Takeaway menu

✣ Provide a prayer card with a prayer you love (perhaps the prayer of St Francis, or the Lord's Prayer). Alternatively, you will be able to purchase resources at your local Christian bookshop.

✣ Choose a landmark near your home that reminds you to say 'hello' to God. For example, it might be a lamp-post or a tree. Use it to remind you to talk to God this month.

✣ In the coming month, sort out all the quarrels and grudges before you go to bed each night.

✣ Find out what sort of food makes everyone in your family feel happy and have a meal that includes everyone's favourite ingredient.

UNIT 10

The story of Esther

This session is the third of three on the theme of women who lived their lives for God.

AIM

To tell the story of Esther and explore how God worked with her to rescue his people.

BIBLE BACKGROUND (Esther 1:1—9:19)

In the right place at the right time

Somewhat like the film *Legally Blonde*, the book of Esther is full of glamour, high life, orphans, evil grand viziers, danger, tension and deeply satisfying retribution—despite the distressingly brutal ending. However, if we are not careful, it is all too easy to focus solely on the glamour side of the story as the beauty treatments, which preceded Esther's fortune in becoming queen of Persia, take over. In fact, the true highlight of the story is God's provision in putting the right person in the right place at the right time and giving her wisdom and courage in the face of mortal danger.

FOOD

Chicken korma

Make up chicken korma as per the instructions on page 68 and serve hot with rice and peas. Put the poppadoms on the table to accompany the meal.

ACTIVITIES

Big picture

You will need: Pictures from the story of Esther, large sheets of paper, pencils, colouring materials (such as paint, pastels or crayons), scissors, PVA glue

Using a web search such as Google images, find a picture of the story of Esther. (If desired, provide two parallel activities, one with a more complicated picture and one with a simpler image.) Print the picture(s) out in colour and cut into about twelve rectangles. Give each person a rectangle that they replicate and enlarge on a larger piece of paper, using paint, pastels, or crayons to complete the work. Stick the finished picture back together like a jigsaw.

Talk about
During this activity, talk about the part of Esther's story featured in the picture.

Beautiful faces

You will need: Paper, pens

On a large piece of paper, have an oval drawn in already, nearly filling the sheet of paper. Invite people to turn their oval into a beautiful face, complete with hair, eyes, ears and so on (and probably nose- or ear-piercings, too, from your teenagers).

Talk about
During this activity, talk about what makes someone beautiful.

Banquet buns

You will need: Buns, icing, decorations

Decorate party buns with mini-marshmallows, sugar strands, sprinkles, buttons and anything else lurid you can track down in the pick 'n' mix department.

Talk about
During this activity, talk about how Esther invited the king to a great feast or party when she wanted to ask a favour of him.

Pamper corner

You will need: Nail varnish, lotion, girly stuff...

Either bring in an expert who can give professional treatments on nails or faces or do it yourself, offering hand massages or simple manicures. Have some wash-off nail varnish, as it may be school tomorrow.

Talk about
During this activity, talk about whether you like people pampering you.

Seaweed wraps

You will need: Green or brown ribbon or paper strips

Wrap a friend in ribbon or paper strips.

Talk about
During this activity, talk about Esther and others undergoing beauty treatments.

Build a throne room

You will need: Junk materials

Provide loads of junk, especially anything on a gold theme, and invite everyone to build a beautiful throne room for a powerful ruler. Ideas might include a throne, wafty fans on poles, treasure chests, 'robot slaves', an indoor bathing pool, a banqueting table and so on.

Talk about
During this activity, talk about how powerful kings were at the time of Esther.

Send a card

You will need: Postcards, stories (either from the Internet or magazines) of people who have been imprisoned

Provide plain postcards and the stories and invite people to decorate and write a postcard, either to the prisoner or to the authorities who are holding them captive.

Talk about
During this activity, talk about the work of organizations like Amnesty International, which stand up for human rights, especially in places where people's voices can't be heard.

Poster noticeboard

You will need: Paper, paints or pens

Design a display in the style of a cinema promotional poster, with the heads of Esther, Xerxes, Mordecai and Haman looking characteristically out of a central point, and with a caption like, 'ESTHER: Can one woman's courage save her people?' or 'ESTHER: when beauty isn't enough…'

Talk about
During this activity, talk about the people in the story to get everyone used to the unusual names.

Crowns, turbans and masks

You will need: Lengths of fabric, card, sequins, tissue paper, sticky tape, PVA glue

Invite people to design a hat for Esther (to make her look ravishingly beautiful), for Xerxes (a kingly crown) or for Haman (something suitable for a powerful prime minister).

Talk about
During this activity, talk about how some people wear hats to show what their job is.

Raspberrying

You will need: Musical instrument basics, balloons, whoopee cushions

Either make some musical instruments from tubes and pots with rice, beans or beads inside to shake, or have fun blowing up balloons and letting the air out to make a raspberry noise. Whoopee cushions could feature in your raucous din.

Talk about
During this activity, talk about the festival of Purim, which the Jewish people still celebrate in March. During the festival, people retell the story of Esther. Every time Haman's name is mentioned in the story, they try to drown it out with as much noise as they can, including anything that makes a rude noise.

CELEBRATION

Songs

✢ Blessed be the name of the Lord (7)
✢ Hands, hands, fingers, thumbs (21)

Show a PowerPoint display of photographs of the session as everyone comes in.

Storytelling

Tell the story of Esther, displaying objects to focus each part of the story as you go along. Someone could bring each object to the front and hold it, or you could simply show pictures of the story on a PowerPoint display. It would also work well as a puppet show with narration. If you have made instruments and have (foolishly) provided whoopee cushions, encourage everyone to drown out the name of Haman each time it is mentioned. Esther's name could be greeted by cheers.

Show some perfume, some bubble bath or a sash.

King Xerxes was a very powerful king of Persia who reigned between 485 and 465BC. One day, in order to choose a new bride, he held a beauty contest. The winner was a Jewish girl named Esther. Esther was an orphan who had been brought up by her cousin, Mordecai, who lived in the capital city of Susa, where the king had his palace.

Show a scroll.

One day, Esther's cousin Mordecai overheard two men plotting to kill the king. He told Esther, who told Xerxes, and the men were put to death. The event was written down in the royal records. King Xerxes had a prime minister called Haman. Haman was so arrogant that he wanted everyone to bow down to him, but Mordecai refused to bow down. Because of this, Haman hated Mordecai and decided to have him killed. Haman knew that Mordecai was Jewish, so he told King Xerxes that people of the Jewish faith didn't obey the law. Haman persuaded the king to order all Jewish people to be killed.

Show a plate of food.

The Jewish people panicked when they heard that they were all going to be put to death. Mordecai sent someone to give a message to

Esther, saying, 'Ask her to go to the king and beg him to have pity on her people, the Jews!' (Esther 4:8). Esther knew that no one could go into the king's presence unless they were called for. Anyone who disobeyed the law risked being killed. However, Esther bravely invited King Xerxes to a banquet to prepare the way to appeal for his help. After the first banquet, she invited him to a second banquet. At both banquets, the only other guest would be the wicked prime minister, Haman. Haman was thrilled and felt very important to be the only person to be invited to a royal banquet. However, he was still angry with Mordecai for refusing to bow down to him. Haman decided to build a tall gallows and hang Mordecai the next day.

Show the scroll again.

That night, the king couldn't sleep, so he had the royal records read out to him. He was reminded of Mordecai's good deed and, in the morning, asked Haman what should be done to honour a really important man. Haman thought the king was talking about him and recommended all the wonderful rewards he would like to receive for himself. Imagine how Haman felt when the king ordered these rewards to be given to Mordecai!

Show a plate of food.

The time came for Esther's second banquet with the king and the wicked prime minister. At the banquet, Esther bravely asked the king to save her and her people. The king didn't know Esther was Jewish and, when he realized that she was one of the people he had ordered to be killed, he was so angry with Haman that he had him killed in the same way that Haman had wanted to kill Mordecai. Although the king couldn't change the order to kill the Jewish people, he did allow them to defend themselves. Sadly, the Jewish people showed little mercy and killed all their enemies while they had the chance. Even today, people still remember Esther for being brave enough to speak up for her people. However, our thoughts of Haman are not so charitable!

Talk in groups about the fact that Esther and Mordecai were the only people in the royal palace who believed in God. Have you ever been in a situation where you are the only one who believes in God? I wonder how we can stand up for people in the places where we are.

Prayer response

Esther used the beauty God had given her to save her people. Let's pray together that God will help us use what he has given us to bring good to people around us.

Leader: Wave your hands… Lord, help us to use our hands with kindness.

Stamp your feet… Lord, help us to go the extra mile for people who need us.

Wiggle your ears… Lord, help us to listen to you and to people who want to talk.

Open and shut your mouth… Lord, help us to speak up for people who need us.

Takeaway menu

✣ Give everyone a sample pack of bubble bath to take home.

✣ Run a luxury bath for someone tired this month.

✣ Pamper each other! Give someone in your family a loving hand massage or paint their toe nails.

✣ Who can you stand up for this month… someone at school or work? Try writing a letter on behalf of a prisoner supported by Amnesty International.

✣ Make a cross out of paper and write on it the names of people in danger. Use the cross over the course of this month to help you to remember to pray for those in danger.

UNIT 11

Who is God?

This unit is one of a series on Christian basics.

AIM

To encourage people to see what God is like through the beauty of the world he created.

BIBLE BACKGROUND (Psalm 19:1)

The wonders of God

Psalm 19 begins with the words, 'The heavens keep telling the wonders of God and the skies declare what he has done.'

One of the ways in which children are very aware of God is through the natural world, so it is good, especially in urban settings, to expose young people to as much nature as you can. You could do this by taking people out into a garden or under a tree, or you might bring nature indoors through natural materials in a flower arrangement or through PowerPoint images. In Psalm 19, the psalmist describes how the skies shout out about God without using words—demonstrating the wonder of non-verbal communication! This session is similar, though not identical, to the unit entitled 'Love your world!' (see pages 92–99), but the focus is on God as creator and sustainer.

FOOD

Pasta twirls

Follow the recipe on page 70 and serve as suggested.

ACTIVITIES

Poppies

You will need: Watercolour paper and paints, brushes

You can create beautiful poppies by painting a vague poppy shape on a piece of watercolour paper with watercolour paint, then dropping into the centre a darker colour and watching it flow into the base colour. Two or three of these on a small rectangle of paper look good enough to frame. Just do the flower, not the stalk.

Talk about
During this activity, talk about colours.

Spinning starbursts

You will need: A paint-spinning machine (available from toy shops or art shops), paint, squares of card

Put a small square of card into the machine, start pressing the button repeatedly and drop different coloured paint into the centre. The paint will whirl out and makes fantastic explosive pictures.

Talk about
During this activity, talk about supernovae and space.

Table decoration

You will need: Dry oasis, a container (such as a margarine lid or similar), florist tape, dried flowers, seed heads, parcel ribbon, florist wire, scissors

Tape oasis on to the container and use a variety of dried wheat, seeds, flowers, bows and so on to decorate it.

Talk about
During this activity, talk about the beautiful flowers and seeds you can find at this time of year: mention the detail of each one.

Seed picture

You will need: Some small rectangular pieces of plastic, card, clear-drying glue, pulses and so on

Find some plastic pieces that will make a nice frame or setting for a piece of coloured card. Paint clear-drying glue on to the card in the shape of a tree or flower and sprinkle on tiny dried peas, lentils or beans, one sort at a time. You can make a lovely fruit tree picture by making the treetop with green beany things and studding orange lentils, or sweetcorn nubs, in among the green.

Talk about
During this activity, talk about the variety of plants in the world.

Gingerbread

You will need: Gingerbread mixture (see recipe on page 70)

Give chunks of gingerbread mixture to people and invite them to create a sun, moon, star or planet. Bake and eat.

Talk about
During this activity, talk about making things with your hands. You might like to have in mind the words of Psalm 8:3a: When I consider your heavens, the work of your fingers...' (NIV).

Starry jewellery

You will need: Star-shaped beads, strong plastic thread, key ring loops

Make bracelets or key rings from star-shaped beads. Craft suppliers can provide not only beads but also strong threading plastic and the wire loops for key rings.

Talk about
During this activity, talk about the beauty of the stars.

Telescopes

You will need: The inner tube from a kitchen roll, pre-painted black, chalk, starry stickers

Decorate the telescope with the stickers. Chalk on the words of Psalm 19:1 (see page 164).

Talk about

During this activity, talk about the constellations, and the animals and people that those who named the constellations saw in them.

Sunrise collage

You will need: Collage materials, strips of coloured paper, PVA glue, scissors, a large sheet of card

Make a collage of a glorious sunrise with different coloured strips of paper.

Talk about

During this activity, talk about the sunrises people have seen.

Junk spaceship

You will need: Big cardboard boxes, tubes and anything shiny and silvery, plus lots of sticky tape

Invite people to make either a handheld spaceship to take home, or an enormous washing machine sized one to enjoy in imaginative play (and to weep over when Mum says they can't take it home—no, really).

Talk about

During this activity, talk about travelling through space.

Quiet corner

You will need: Rugs, cushions, picture books, pens or pencils, sheets of paper, sheer fabrics, tealight candles (optional)

Not a craft activity, but as a first step to putting more emphasis on the spiritual, create a quiet space with rugs, cushions, picture books to look at and a prayer activity to do quietly. Use sheer fabrics to create a 'beach shelter' tent affair, which gives a very useful sense of being enclosed without hiding misdemeanours from view. If your décor permits, you might experiment with one of the popular mosquito nets that go over children's beds, or praying with candles if they can be adequately supervised. (One of our parents said, 'If I'd known you were doing that, I'd have brought my three-year-old—he would love it.')

Talk about
During this activity, talk about the benefit of creating a quiet space to be with God.

CELEBRATION

Songs

✤ Father God I wonder (17)
✤ Have we made our God too small? (23)
✤ King of love (50)
✤ Our God is a great big God (from *Great Big God*, Volume 1).

As everyone comes in, show a PowerPoint display of the different crafts people have made, with the soundtrack of 'What a wonderful world' by Louis Armstrong.

Storytelling

To help illustrate the theme, search on the Internet for 'space pictures', 'NASA images', 'Hubble images' or similar. The Hubble Heritage website has a fun 'Pan and zoom gallery'. Several websites have videos or animations of things happening in space to download and play.

Talk about the crafts and how we can sometimes tell a little about the person who made something by the thing they made. Show a picture or sculpture you have at home or at church, and ask what you can tell about the person who made it. Say:

I wonder what you can tell about God from the universe he has made. Perhaps we can think about how big God is.

Ask people to hold different balls to represent the earth, the sun, the moon and Alpha Centauri. Arrange the first three in suitably close together positions.

Where do you think Alpha Centauri—our nearest star after the sun— should stand in relation to the moon and the sun? On the same scale, the person holding Alpha Centauri would have to go all the way to Paris and stand by the Eiffel Tower! The universe is huge… so what is the Maker of the universe like?

But Bible tells us that God also made human beings. Can you count the hairs on your head? Jesus says your heavenly Father knows you in so much detail that he even knows how many hairs you have on your head. He might be huge, but he cares about every single detail of our lives. How amazing is that!

As we sometimes sing, 'Our God is a great big God and he holds us in his hand.'

Prayer response

Invite everyone to hold out their arms as wide as they can.

Leader: Thank you, Creator God, for being bigger than we can possibly imagine. Show your amazing power in the lives of people who are unwell and in countries at war, such as...

Invite everyone to hold their fingers as if they have a tiny thing between their fingertips.

Leader: Thank you, Lord God, that you love every detail about us and that you care about everything we do.

Takeaway menu

✢ Go and look at the clouds or a sunset or the stars together. Take some doughnuts and drinking chocolate with you.
✢ Collect things from the park or your garden, and make a collage out of them for the kitchen wall.
✢ Read one of the stories of God making the world, from Genesis 1:1—2:4.
✢ Say a 'thank you' prayer at bedtime for all the beautiful things you have seen today.

UNIT 12

Who is Jesus?

This unit is one in a series on Christian basics.

AIM

To tell the big story of Jesus.

BIBLE BACKGROUND (The four Gospels)

The story of recreation

The crafts in this unit may seem disparate and unconnected, but everything comes together in the story of recreation at the celebration, in which each craft activity links into Jesus' work of putting the world back together. One way to approach Jesus' life on earth is to see him as a 'mender' coming to mend a broken world— first of all by healing, then through the mystery of the cross, then in partnership with his people through the Holy Spirit. Often, when we look at individual events in Jesus' life, we only get a fragmented view of Jesus. However, the story of recreation draws together the big picture of his life.

FOOD

Shepherd's pie

Make up a mince-based sauce. Top with mashed potato and, if desired, grated cheese. Bake in a hot oven for 30 minutes. Serve with vegetables or baked beans.

ACTIVITIES

Get well card

You will need: Card-making equipment, PVA glue, scissors, pencils and felt-tipped pens, envelopes

Make a simple card, such as shapes stuck on to a folded card, or a more complicated pop-up card, or something on a concertina paper spring that jumps out when you open it. Invite people to make the card for someone they know who isn't well and to send it to them.

Talk about
During this activity, talk about how God wants everyone to be 'mended' and made better from their illnesses.

My book of Jesus

You will need: Paper, card, copies of pictures from Jesus' life, stapler, felt-tipped pens

Which stories of Jesus do you think are most important? Which would you include in a book about Jesus? Choose five pictures to colour and put together as your book about Jesus, and design a cover for it. If there isn't a picture of a story you want to include, draw your own.

Talk about
During this activity, talk about the Gospel writers: Matthew, Mark, Luke and John.

Nest and bird

You will need: Rice crispies, chocolate, marzipan, bun cases

Melt the chocolate and stir in the rice crispies. Mould the mixture into a nest shape in a bun case. While it is setting, make a bird out of a blob of marzipan, then put the bird safely in its nest.

Talk about
During this activity, talk about how much God loves us—even more than he loves the sparrows or other 'birds of the air' (Luke 12:6–7; Matthew 6:25–26).

Growing love

You will need: Kitchen roll, scissors, cress seeds, lids or shallow containers, water

Cut a heart shape out of the kitchen roll and place it in the lid, then sprinkle on some cress seeds and dampen the whole thing.

Talk about
During this activity, talk about how stories about Jesus fall like seeds into people's hearts and grow as the people grow up, changing the way they live. (Mark 4:1–20 talks about the word of God being like seeds scattered in a field.)

Junk boats

You will need: Junk and sticky tape, a child's paddling pool filled with water

Make junk boats and either invite people to test the seaworthiness of their vessels or have a competition to see which boats float best.

Talk about
During this activity, talk about the story of Jesus calming the storm (Mark 4:35–41).

Quilled crosses

You will need: Crosses cut from sturdy card, quilling tools, very narrow strips of paper in different colours, PVA glue

Choose five colours of paper and use the quilling tool to roll the narrow strip of paper into a very tight roll. Glue it on to the cross in the centre and in the places where Jesus' head, hands and feet were. Older people could then add different shapes made out of quilled rolls by experimenting with letting them unravel a little or pressing them into ovals or teardrop shapes.

Talk about
During this activity, talk about the people who love you and how you know they do.

Sunrise picture

You will need: Ruler, pencil, circles cut from bright yellow paper for the sun, a selection of papers and tissue paper, corrugated paper, collage scraps, PVA glue

Divide a piece of paper roughly in half lengthways with a faint pencil line, and place the paper in front of you so that the line is horizontal. Above the pencil line, glue strips of bright coloured paper for the sky. Glue on the sun circle. Then, using different sorts of paper, glue on shapes for the landscape in the foreground to represent hills, with stripes in greens, browns and greys. If desired, you could glue the cross from the previous activity on to the landscape.

Talk about
During this activity, talk about new starts.

'Who is Jesus?' display

You will need: A large cut-out silhouette of Jesus, a large sheet of card, PVA glue, coloured pastel crayons

Stick the silhouette of Jesus on the sheet of card. Invite people to draw or write on Jesus' robes their answer to the question, 'Who is Jesus?'

Talk about
During this activity, talk about the time when Jesus asked his disciples, 'Who do you say I am?' (Mark 8:29). Who do you think Jesus is?

Decorated shoeboxes

You will need: Empty shoeboxes in good condition, fliers from a charity that operates a shoebox appeal (such as Samaritan's Purse), wrapping paper, sticky tape, scissors

The 'Send a shoebox' appeal is an excellent idea, but for some people it's hard to find time to obtain and decorate a shoebox. Provide and decorate the shoebox at Messy Church and half the job is done.

Talk about
During this activity, talk about the charities that allow us to send presents to children who would otherwise have no presents at Christmas.

Painting Jesus

You will need: Pictures of Jesus from other cultures (the resource pack *The Christ We Share* is published by CMS, USPG and The Methodist Church, available from www.cms-shop.org.uk), paints, brushes, paper

Paint your picture of Jesus. This sounds simple, and it is, and we've had some spectacular surprises with the results.

Talk about
During this activity, talk about how different people see Jesus.

CELEBRATION

Songs

- ✢ All right now (3)
- ✢ Lord, I lift your name on high (59)
- ✢ Oh it's great great brill brill (66)
- ✢ We want to see Jesus lifted high (92)

Show a PowerPoint display of photographs of the craft activities as everyone comes in.

Storytelling

This story of recreation was written by Martyn Payne. It is modelled on the methodology of *Godly Play*. If you are familiar with the story of creation by Jerome Berryman (see www.godlyplay.com), you'll hear echoes.

The story of recreation

You will need:
- ✢ A background cloth of dark blue felt about 1m to 1.5m long and 20–30cm wide
- ✢ A baby in a manger
- ✢ A dove (a small portion of white feather boa will suffice)
- ✢ Three seeds
- ✢ Three green leaves

✛ A tealight candle
✛ A box of matches (or a candle lighter)
✛ A model bird
✛ A boat
✛ A cross
✛ A risen Jesus figure (such as a wooden 'people of God' figure available from St Michael's Cottage Crafts; telephone: 01603 746106)
✛ Figures to represent Christians (such as the 'people of God' figures available as above)
✛ Squares or rectangles of felt to lie on the felt backdrop for four 'portions' of the story (two in pale blue and two in green). When the story is complete, the backgrounds of the seven sections should be (from your right to your left) dark blue, light blue, green, dark blue, light blue, green, dark blue).

Place down the backcloth, rolled up so that it can be unrolled from your right to your left (so that the audience sees from left to right). Unroll one portion.

In the beginning—in the second beginning—there was a baby.

Place the baby in the manger on the unrolled portion of the cloth.

The baby was the light for the world, the light that all light came from. Mary and Joseph held him close and kept him safe and watched him grow.

Unroll the second portion and place down the first blue square.

When Jesus was about 30 years old, he went down to the River Jordan where his cousin John was baptizing people. John took Jesus down into the water and Jesus came up into the light. And some people said they saw what appeared to be a dove come down from heaven and rest on Jesus.

Place the dove on the blue square.

Other people said they heard a voice from heaven, which said, 'You are my own dear Son, and I am pleased with you.'

Unroll the third portion and place down the first green square. As you speak, place down three seeds, then three leaves.

Now it was time for Jesus to begin his work. But what was his work? His work was to mend what was broken, to put the world together again. His work was to tell stories. The stories fell like seeds, not into the ground but into people's hearts, where they grew and changed and helped people know more about God, more about each other and more about the kingdom of heaven.

Unroll the fourth portion and, as you speak, light a tealight candle and place it down.

What was his work? His work was to lighten the darkness. Jesus came close to people whom no one else would come close to. When he was near them, they changed. They could see things they couldn't see before. They could do things they couldn't do before. They were healed.

Unroll the fifth portion and place the second blue square on it. As you speak, place first a bird, then a boat, on the square.

What was his work? His work was to tell people how much God loves them—that he loves them even more than he loves the birds of the air (and he loves the birds very much). And that when our lives feel like a tiny boat tossed on the waves, Jesus can come close and say, 'Peace, be still', and we can know the deep-down peace he brings.

Unroll the sixth portion and place the second green square on it. As you speak, place a cross on the square.

Finally, the time came for Jesus to go up to Jerusalem for the last time. He knew that the only way to mend the world and put right what had been broken was to stretch himself out between heaven and earth and to die on a cross. On the cross, Jesus brought God and people back together, and people back together with each other.

Unroll the seventh portion and place down the 'people of God' figures as you speak.

But, three days later, people saw Jesus alive again. Now anyone can share in his work to mend the world, to put right what has been broken—on and on into the future, for as long as time lasts. And all this began with a baby at Christmas.

✢ I wonder which part of this story you like best.
✢ I wonder which part you want to take away with you today.

Prayer response

Invite people to think of something they know that is broken and needs mending. Say that Jesus wants to mend all of us so that we are as good as new.

Leader: Dear Jesus, please mend our bodies, our minds and our hearts. Please mend our friendships when they get broken and help us to mend your world, too.

Takeaway menu

✣ At home, find something that has been broken for a long time and mend it so that it is useful again.

✣ In a Bible, find the Gospel stories that were mentioned in the story of recreation: the Christmas story, Jesus' baptism, a parable, a healing miracle, what Jesus said about the birds of the air, the calming of the storm, his death and his coming back to life. Read them to each other. If you can't find them, email your minister.

✣ Look out for broken friendships at school and at work, and think what you can do to help mend them.

✣ Think of someone you don't like much or someone you have quarrelled with, and secretly give them a Mars Bar. Ssssh, don't tell them it's from you!

UNIT 13

Who is the Holy Spirit?

This unit is one of a series on Christian basics.

AIM

To find out about the Holy Spirit's character.

BIBLE BACKGROUND (Galatians 5:22–23)

Aspects of love

Often there is a tendency to focus on the Holy Spirit only in the context of Pentecost, which highlights the dramatic events of wind, fire and speaking in foreign languages. Concentrating on Pentecost means that the more gentle aspects of the Holy Spirit's character—those that enable us daily to grow more like Jesus—can be overlooked. The image of the fruit of God's Spirit is something to be built into everyday life—a complementary aspect of the Holy Spirit's work alongside the more dramatic images of Pentecost.

FOOD

Hotdogs and wedges

See page 70 for details of the recipe and serving suggestions.

ACTIVITIES

Fruity mobile

You will need: Either pea sticks fastened together with a twist of wire or a wire coat hanger, coloured paper, marker pens or metallic pens, scissors, thread, a list of the fruits of the Spirit from Galatians 5:23–23 ('loving, happy, peaceful, patient, kind, good, faithful, gentle and self-controlled')

Have some fruit templates to choose from. To make a fruit, cut out two fruit shapes and colour them in. Using a marker pen or metallic pen, write one of the fruits of the Spirit in several places on the fruit. Next, cut vertically to a central point on one shape from the bottom and on the other from the top. The two pieces should then slot together to make a 3D fruit, which can be strung on to the coat hanger. People could make one mobile each to take home, or everyone could make one together, with a cornucopia of fruit hanging from it, to display in the Messy Church venue.

Talk about
During this activity, talk about the way a tree produces fruit and the way that the Holy Spirit produces fruit in our lives.

Fruit salad bowls

You will need: Vegetable knives, chopping boards, oranges, a selection of other fruits (as wide a variety as you can find)

Cut the oranges in half and scoop out the insides. Chop up the other fruit and put pieces of lots of different sorts in your orange skin bowl.

NB: For safety reasons, keep a count of how many knives you have out, and supervise younger children.

Talk about
During this activity, talk about healthy eating—for our bodies as well as for our souls and minds.

Fruit tree

You will need: A large branch firmly stuck into a flower pot to look like a tree, funky art foam or card, sequins, pens, PVA glue, scissors, thread

Make an art foam fruit for the tree, choose which fruit of the Spirit to let it symbolize, write the name on the fruit and decorate with sequins or shapes from the cut-out art foam scraps. Hang the fruit from the tree with thread.

Talk about
During this activity, talk about any fruit trees growing in your neighbourhood.

Fruit badge

You will need: Fruit-scented felt-tipped pens, card, safety pins, scissors

Choose a fruit of the Spirit that you would most like to grow in your life. Write it on the badge with a scented felt-tipped pen and decorate the rest of the badge using scented felt-tips.

Talk about

During this activity, talk about how you might explain to someone what your badge is all about.

Perfumed bath salts

You will need: Scented bath salts of different sorts, lidded pots, flower petals, water

Make up your own scented bath salts by mixing different scents together. Take home in a pot with a lid. Younger people might also enjoy making their own 'perfume' by stirring up flower petals and water.

Talk about

During this activity, talk about how things can be real even if you can't see them—you can sense them in other ways.

Windy day display

You will need: A tree painted on to a display board, leaves (real ones), PVA glue or a stapler

Invite people to simply stick a leaf on the tree to show that a powerful wind is blowing.

Talk about

During this activity, talk about how we know the wind is there. Can you see the wind?

Firework splatter painting

You will need: Dark paper, paintbrushes, paint, plastic sheeting

Cover the activity area with plastic sheeting. Invite people to make firework pictures by dipping a paintbrush into paint and flicking it over the paper, or running their fingers over the bristles to flick it. Experiment with thinner and thicker paints.

Talk about
During this activity, talk about fire—one of the symbols for the Holy Spirit. Fire, in the form of fireworks, can be fun and exciting.

Seal of belonging

You will need: Sealing wax, matches, certificates, a seal of some sort (you can buy little kits containing a seal and wax from larger stationers or craft shops)

Pre-print some certificates with wording such as:

I

....

belong to Jesus.

Signed and sealed this .... day

of .... 20......

Drip some wax on to the certificate (it's best if an older person does this as the angle is tricky to judge when you're young) and make an impression with the seal next to your signature.

NB: Take care not to burn your fingers on the hot wax.

Talk about
During this activity, talk about how the Bible describes the Holy Spirit as a seal to guarantee that Jesus is living in us (2 Corinthians 1:22; Ephesians 1:13–14). In olden days, people would prove a document was genuine by stamping their seal ring into some wax.

Bubbles

You will need: Pots of bubble mix, plastic sheeting

Cover the activity area with plastic sheeting (as the floor will soon become slippery). Have a happy time blowing bubbles and popping them.

Talk about
During this activity, talk about the way the Holy Spirit fills us, like our breath fills the bubble mixture.

Filled to the brim

You will need: Cigar-shaped ice cream wafer tubes, Angel Delight-type dessert mix, milk, a whisk, icing piping bag kit

Invite people to examine the wafer tubes to see how hollow they are and how there is a big space that could be filled with something good. Make up the mix together, put it into the piping bag and fill up a wafer tube with the dessert.

Talk about
During this activity, talk about the way Jesus wants to fill us up with his Holy Spirit.

CELEBRATION

Songs

✤ I wanna be a bloomin tree (34)
✤ May the God of hope (61)
✤ There is a God (84)

Show a PowerPoint display of photographs of the session as everyone comes in.

Storytelling

Invite someone to give a personal account of the ways they have seen the Holy Spirit at work in their own life or in the lives of others. You may have someone in your church or team who has a story to tell, perhaps from an Alpha weekend or just an everyday happening.

Prayer response

Say that Jesus loves us to be filled with the Holy Spirit, just as Adam, the first person whom God created, was filled with the breath of God (Genesis 2:7). Invite everyone to watch you blow a bubble and, as you blow into the mixture, invite everyone to breathe in as a sign that they would also like God's Holy Spirit. As the bubble floats away, breathe out again.

Leader: Dear Jesus, thank you that you are part of our lives through your Holy Spirit. Come into every part of our lives today.

Takeaway menu

✣ On the next windy day, go out and blow dandelion clocks into the wind, fly a kite, or feel the wind on your face.
✣ Pray that each person in your home will be filled with the Holy Spirit.
✣ Make meringues (they are full of air). Fill with whipped cream. Take one as a present to someone.
✣ Collect some money for an asthma charity.

UNIT 14

Messy baptism

This unit is a stand-alone session, designed to explore what it means to belong to the family of God, but also for use in the event of a baptism taking place at Messy Church.

AIM

To think about promises, especially Jesus' words, 'I will be with you always, even until the end of the world' (Matthew 28:20).

BIBLE BACKGROUND (Ephesians 4:4–5)

One Lord, one faith, one baptism

The exciting thing about the Christian faith is that it is not so much about who we are as who God is. Through Jesus, and because of God's grace and loving kindness towards us, we are all invited to be part of his family. Baptism is a sign of our belonging to the worldwide family of God.

FOOD

Turkey casserole

Spread out turkey pieces (and sliced vegetables if desired) in casserole dishes. Pour tins of mushroom or chicken soup over them. Bake in a hot oven for approximately one hour. Have a quorn option available for vegetarians. Serve with mashed potato and peas.

ACTIVITIES

Heart badge

You will need: Card, pens or pencils, decorations, clear plastic, safety pins, sticky tape

Design a heart-shaped badge on sturdy card and attach a safety pin to the back. Covering it with clear plastic film can make it look more professional.

Talk about
During this activity, talk about God's love, which is with us before our birth and beyond our death.

Cross in my pocket

You will need: Plastic tapestry mesh, tapestry needles, embroidery thread or tapestry wool, scissors

Make a cross for your pocket to remind you that God is with you everywhere. Cut a cross shape out of the plastic tapestry mesh and sew bright wool across the squares in cross-stitch or diagonal stitches.

Talk about
During this activity, talk about remembering that God is near us wherever we are.

Sand footprints

You will need: Paper, pencils, PVA glue, silver sand (available from toy shops), a sand tray (optional), bowls of soapy water and paper towels

Either draw round your foot and fill in the outline with glue, then scatter sand on it, or paint glue on your foot, stand on the paper to leave a print and scatter sand on that. You could also have fun walking in the sand tray if the sand is slightly damp. Provide soapy water and paper towels for people to clean and dry their feet.

Talk about
During this activity, talk about the well-known 'Footprints' poem, about a dream of Jesus walking beside a person on a beach (authorship disputed). Copies of the poem are available from Christian bookshops on cards, tea towels, bookmarks—and probably imprinted on socks, vests and swimwear by now.

Footprints cards

You will need: A5 medium-weight card, scissors, the 'Footprints' poem (see above), foot-shaped craft punch, PVA glue

Have the 'Footprints' poem printed out on cards (see above). Invite people to decorate their card with footprints. (You can buy small foot-shaped craft punches from craft shops or Internet sites, such as www.stamps.co.uk, or www.artymiss.co.uk.) Use either the holes or the cut-outs or both to decorate the cards.

Talk about
During this activity, talk about the story above.

Friendship bracelets

You will need: Embroidery threads, scissors, sticky tape

Make friendship bracelets. Instructions can be found on the Internet or in a craft book. Make the suggestion that people could give the bracelet to a friend.

Talk about
During this activity, talk about Jesus being the best friend we will ever have, and the fact that he will never leave us.

'Nothing can separate us from God's love' noticeboard

You will need: A large sheet of card, pens, paints, paintbrushes

Design a noticeboard using the words from Romans 8:38 (see above) as the central focus. Invite people to decorate the board with images of what Paul's words mean to them.

Talk about
During this activity, talk about Paul's beautiful words in Romans 8:38–39, and his certainty that nothing can ever separate us from God's love.

Marbling

You will need: Marbling inks, water in a shallow bowl, stirrers, paper

Invest in some good-quality marbling inks (they seem expensive compared with paints, but they last for ages and are fabulous). Shake the bottles well and drop a few drops on to the surface of a shallow bowl of water. Drop some paper down flat on top of the surface and whisk it straight off. When it is dry, the paper can be used as writing paper, bookplates, bookmarks, or similar.

Talk about
During this activity, talk about the way that Jesus wants our life to be in his, and his in ours, like two colours marbled together to make something beautiful.

Mirror prints

You will need: Paper, paints, paintbrushes

Fold a piece of paper in half, open it up and paint shapes or patterns on one half. While the paint is still wet, fold the paper back in half so that the empty half is printed on by the painted half. Open it up and see the new pattern it makes.

Talk about
During this activity, talk about how we are made in the image of God.

Edible candle

You will need: Fondant icing, biscuits, liquorice laces, almonds, satsuma oranges

Make an edible candle by using a biscuit as the base and adding a cylinder of white fondant icing wrapped round a liquorice lace 'wick' that just sticks out of one end. Finish with a flame made from either an almond or an upended satsuma segment (you will need to push the almond or satsuma into the icing to hold it upright).

Talk about
During this activity, talk about the way we give a candle to someone who has been baptized to show that they have gone from darkness into light.

Free-range junk

You will need: Junk, sticky tape, scissors, PVA glue, string

There are often times when cupboards at home need a clear-out. Seek out all the odds and ends of junk and bring them along to Messy Church. Leave them out on the floor with glue, sticky tape, scissors and string for free-range junk modelling. What can you make?

Talk about
During this activity, talk about the fun of making things.

CELEBRATION

Songs

✢ I'm forever in your love (39)
✢ Waterfall (89)

Show a PowerPoint display of photographs of the session as everyone comes in.

Storytelling

You may belong to a church that has certain definite requirements for the wording of the baptism service. You may, however, have permission to be more flexible with the service. Below are some creative suggestions to make the most of the service.

Symbolism

How can you make the most of the wonderful symbolism? Focus on the symbolism of the water as something that gives life, cleanses and refreshes. Include as many visuals and other references to water as you can imagine and as are suitable for your setting. For example, bottles of water around the front of your venue, an electronic water feature (switched on), watering cans, a hosepipe, large bowls of water reflecting the surroundings, long strips of blue or green cloth running up the alleyways or aisles, PowerPoint pictures of different sorts of watery scenes. There might be scope for sprinkling everyone with water, or spraying them using a small water pistol, at some point in the celebration. Any prayers that you include might involve water in some way, such as dropping stones into water, or the words of the prayer displayed on a background of watery scenes. If you use a service order, you could include pictures of water.

Movement

How can you make the most of the possibilities for movement? Fonts in churches were traditionally placed near the door to symbolize entering the Christian life, just as you enter the building. Build in a journey from one part of the room you are using to another, to symbolize moving on in faith. If you move during the songs, it means that you will not be slowing the celebration down.

Participation

How can you build in as much participation as possible? Parts of the Anglican service involve the candidates for baptism responding to questions. Consider inviting everyone to join in with the responses to those questions. This will help anyone at the front of church who is shy, and it will give everyone a chance either to renew their own commitment or to practise what they might be saying themselves one day at their own baptism.

Participation could also be built in with opportunities for different people to bring forward the water, to pour it, to light candles and to pray blessings over the people being baptized or to say parts of the service that don't need to be spoken by the authorized minister. Imagine how moving it would be to have the prayer of blessing after baptism, for example, spoken by a child or a godparent.

There are also opportunities for participation in the welcome you give to the newly baptized people. Instead of just saying, 'We welcome you…' you could add a physical movement, either formalized or informal, depending on your setting—such as a hug, a group hug, a cheer or an opportunity to shake hands. If candles or copies of a Gospel are given as gifts, perhaps different people could make the presentation.

Words

You may wish to consider cutting down the wording of the set liturgy to its bare minimum and, if absolutely necessary, building up from there. Often, we tend to be a bit hung up on words and gleefully splurge as many words as possible. But 'less not more' works best with all-age services, and silence is golden. A pause in the speaking, for example, while water is reverently poured can communicate a great deal.

Prayer response

Use the set prayers in your church's baptism liturgy, or make up your own based on the symbolism demonstrated in the crafts and the creative suggestions in the celebration.

Takeaway menu

✢ If anyone in your family has been baptized, find the photos and talk about the celebration you had on that day.
✢ Play with some water, inside or out.
✢ Collect some money for a charity that provides clean drinking water for people in another part of the world.
✢ Pour some iced water into your most beautiful glasses and say 'thank you' to God for the gift of water before you drink it.

UNIT 15

Messy Communion

This unit is a stand-alone session, designed to explore the significance of the sacrament of Holy Communion, but also for use in the event of a service of Holy Communion taking place at Messy Church.

AIM

To enjoy a service of Holy Communion together.

BIBLE BACKGROUND
(Matthew 26:17–30; Luke 22:19–20;
1 Corinthians 11:23–26)

Holy Communion

Jesus gave his followers the gift of a meal by which to remember his death and resurrection, a meal he first shared with his close friends just before he died. The early Church evidently carried on celebrating it together, as we see in 1 Corinthians 11:23–26. Today, Christians at different points on their spiritual journey share it, enjoy it and understand it in different ways and for different reasons. Jesus invited his followers to remember him through this meal (Luke 22:19–20) and the Church continues to extend that invitation. The bread and wine have remained an effective and tangible sign of Jesus' love for over 2000 years.

FOOD

Pasta twirls

Cook the pasta and make up the recipe using the instructions on page 70. Serve with grated cheese, cucumber sticks, cold sweetcorn and French bread.

ACTIVITIES

At each of the activities today, have the means to wash and dry hands. As a reminder of Jesus washing his friends' feet, invite people to allow the leaders to wash and dry each person's hands after each activity.

Prayer tree

You will need: A branch set in a plant pot, coloured paper, thread, a hole punch, pens, scissors

Invite people to draw and cut out leaves and to write on them intercessory prayers for other people, places in the world or the Church. Punch a hole in one end of the leaf and hang it on the tree, using thread if necessary.

Talk about
During this activity, talk about the different things we can pray for.

Altar cloth

You will need: A plain tablecloth, scraps of coloured fabric, fabric pens, glittery embroidery threads, embroidery needles, felt squares, PVA glue, scissors, sewing thread, coloured fabrics cut into small pieces (mosaics)

You could turn this into an activity that would occupy the entire hour over several months and make something beautiful and long-lasting, or you could make something meant to be used just for today. Here are some ideas for the latter.

Spread out the tablecloth and ask everyone to sign it or draw a picture of themselves with a fabric pen. Older people could embroider over the top of their signature with glittery thread. Have simple felt cut-outs of different body and head shapes for people to select, glue together and personalize to look like themselves. Stitch the felt figures to the cloth. Give everyone a square of coloured fabric in different shades and invite them to decorate their square to be personal to them. Stitch the finished squares on to the cloth. Finally, draw a basic patterned outline on the borders of the cloth and invite everyone to help glue on different coloured fabric pieces to make a mosaic pattern. Depending on your requirement, the finished cloth could be a tablecloth, altar frontal or rug to sit round.

Talk about

During this activity, talk about the way some people eat around a table, others eat sitting on the floor, and others sit on the sofa to eat.

Candles

You will need: A candle-making kit (a non-heating version, such as sheets of beeswax to roll into a candle shape, is safest)

Make some candles to use in the worship, or, if you think people will want to take their candle away, make a candle of your own that is identical to the ones you will use in worship.

A more complex but effective candle is an ice candle. This is an activity that involves pouring hot wax, so it might be one for older children and adults only, under close supervision.

You will need: Small candle moulds (small so that the candles take less time to cool and set), wicks, pencils or small sticks to tie the wicks and keep them taut, seal (such as Blu-Tack), melted-down candle wax, or wax nuggets and stearin mix (10% stearin to 90% wax), ice cubes

Thread the wick into the mould and secure the small hole with a seal such as Blu-Tack. Tighten the wick so that it goes straight down the middle of the mould and tie it on to the pencil or stick that is placed across the wider opening at the top of the mould. Place the mould in a heatproof tray or bowl.

Melt the wax in a bain-marie (not over a direct heat source). Fill the mould with ice cubes. Carefully pour the molten wax over the ice cubes until the mould is full and leave to set. Remove the mould over a sink as the ice will have melted and the wax will have set around the cavities it leaves, in unique formations.

Talk about
During this activity, talk about the way Christians use candles in worship, often to symbolize Jesus as the light for the world.

Bread

You will need: Bread-making ingredients and equipment (see recipe on page 71)

Ideally together, make a loaf to be used in the worship. If there isn't time, make individual rolls, which take less time to cook, in the shape and style of the one that you will use in the worship.

Talk about

During this activity, talk about what Jesus meant when he said he was the bread that gives life (John 6:35).

Non-alcoholic wine

You will need: Clean hands, grapes, spoons, bowls or a press

Give each person a few grapes and invite them to press the juice out of them. They will only squeeze out a few drops, but that doesn't matter. Collect the drops together in a jug to be used in the worship.

Talk about

During this activity, talk about what Jesus meant when he said he was the true vine (John 15:1).

Plate

You will need: A plastic plate large enough to hold the loaf you are making, a clear plastic plate or clingfilm (if you are concerned that the decorations may stick to the food on the plate), flour and water paste or non-toxic glue, coloured magazines, scissors

Decorate the plate together (or decorate your own plate in similar style) with pictures of good food cut carefully out of magazines and glued on to the plate to overlap and cover it completely. If there isn't much time for the decoration to dry, cover it with clingfilm or a clear plastic plate before you use it in the worship.

Talk about
During this activity, talk about the food you enjoy eating on special occasions.

Cup

You will need: A goblet-style glass with a base, PVA glue, small squares of coloured paper or beads

Decorate the base of the goblet with the mosaic pieces and put a few round the outside of the cup part of the goblet. (Don't cover the entire cup as they might make it hard to hold, especially if the glue is still tacky and apt to slide.)

Talk about
During this activity, talk about celebration drinks.

Polishing the silver

You will need: Appropriate silver polish and cloths, the church silver

If you have some, you might prefer to use the usual church silver for your service. Polishing silver can be great fun and also gives a sense of ownership.

Talk about
During this activity, talk about treasures.

Resurrection surrounding banner

You will need: A long roll of plain paper, such as lining wallpaper (not ready-pasted), paints, sponges, pencils

The idea is to make a mural that surrounds everyone during the service. The mural shows images of the last supper, Jesus' death and resurrection, and the coming of the Holy Spirit. Divide the paper into four and either provide a basic drawing in each section for people to sponge-paint or invite everyone to fill each section with their own images of the last supper, Jesus' death and resurrection, and the coming of the Holy Spirit.

Talk about
During this activity, talk about the Easter story.

'Be prepared' kit

You will need: Stickers, pen, small box, strong envelope or self-sealing plastic bag, plaster, small pencils (these can be long pencils broken into three pieces and sharpened), paper, string, 20p pieces, tissues, paperclip, toothpick, other 'emergency' requirements

It is good to be prepared for emergencies. It is also good to be ready for things to happen. Make up a little kit of things that could be useful in an emergency. What might each part of this kit be useful for? Older people could write or type a list of instructions. Design a sticker to go on the front of the kit.

Talk about
During this activity, talk about the way we get ready to meet God. Isaiah talked about John the Baptist getting people ready to meet Jesus by declaring, 'Turn back to God! The kingdom of heaven will soon be here' (Matthew 3:2). We often need to get ready for important days.

Table

You will need: Some thin rope (or strong string), wooden poles (or sawn planks), someone who knows how to do lashing (see www.scoutingresources.org.uk for further information about lashing and knots)

Construct a table for Communion.

Talk about
During this activity, talk about the stability of the table and how to keep it upright.

CELEBRATION

Setting up the church

Install the table and the mural beforehand. At the door of the church or room, gather together the objects that will be used in the celebration and give them to members of the congregation to carry in. Ask both adults and children to bring things in.

Leader: We're about to celebrate a special meal together, as Jesus' friends have done for thousands of years. If you are able, say, 'We're ready!' to the questions I am about to ask. Are you ready to celebrate?

All: We're ready!

Leader: We're about to do what Jesus told us to do to remember him. Are you ready to remember him?

All: We're ready!

Leader: In the name of the Father and the Son and the Holy Spirit, are you ready?

All: We're ready!

Leader: Then let's go!

The leader invites everyone to hold someone else's hand as they come in— a friend or member of their family—so that no one is on their own. Everyone walks together to the seats, singing a simple repetitive song that doesn't require words to be displayed, such as 'Father, we love you… (Jesus, we love you… Spirit, we love you…)'. Gather around the table in a circle. It might help to have some 'stewards' to guide people to their places.

Leader: The table needs to be got ready for our special remembering meal. Let's bring up the things we need.

Members of the congregation bring up the candle, cup, plate, bread, wine and prayers on the prayer tree. The leader describes each item briefly and places them on the table.

Leader: And now the table is ready.

So that we are ready on the inside, too, we need to say 'sorry' to God for the wrong things we have thought, said and done. We also need to say 'sorry' for all the good things we haven't done. In a moment of quiet, let us tell God what we are sorry for, and ask for his forgiveness. Please respond with the words, 'Thank you, Lord' after this short prayer. Dear God, we are very sorry for the wrong things we have done. For forgiving us all...

All: Thank you, Lord.

Leader: Now we are ready to remember Jesus.

Father God, we remember that on the night before he died Jesus had supper with his friends. Taking some bread, he praised you, broke the bread, gave it to them and said, 'This is my body, which is given for you. Eat this and remember me.'

When supper was ended, Jesus took the cup of wine. Again he praised you, gave it to his friends and said, 'This is my blood, and with it God makes his new agreement with you. Drink this and remember me.'

All: Jesus has died, *(repeat)*

Jesus is risen,

Jesus will come again.

The leader explains how the bread and wine—or grape juice—will be distributed, and that those who do not yet receive the bread and wine will be offered a blessing instead, or whatever procedure is appropriate in your situation.

Play a quiet song, such as 'Broken for me', either on a CD or 'live', during the distribution of the bread and wine.

Leader: Dear God, for all you give us...

All: Thank you, Lord.

Leader: For giving us our family to love and to love us...

All: Thank you, Lord.

Leader: For giving us yourself...
All: Thank you, Lord.
Leader: Let's say the grace together with our usual actions. *(Explain actions if necessary.)*
All: May the grace of our Lord Jesus Christ... *(Hold out hands to receive)*
And the love of God... *(Cross arms on chest)*
And the fellowship of the Holy Spirit... *(Hold hands with neighbours)*
Be with us all, evermore. Amen *(Raise hands in the air together)*
Leader: And now let us thank God for the tea we are about to eat.

Everyone goes out together.

Takeaway menu

✛ Read the story of the last supper from a children's Bible.
✛ Jesus washed his friends' feet before the meal to show them that they should serve one another rather than be waited on. Do a job this week at home, school or work which usually you would let someone else do for you.
✛ Say grace before one meal a day this week.
✛ Have hot buttered toast together when you come in from school or work one day this week.

Index of activities

FOOD-BASED ACTIVITIES

CRAFT-BASED ACTIVITIES

JUNK CRAFTS

COLLAGES AND DISPLAYS

SPECIAL INTEREST ACTIVITIES

JUST FOR FUN

Bible index

OLD TESTAMENT

ALSO BY LUCY MOORE

Messy Church

Fresh ideas for building a Christ-centred community

Messy Church is bursting with easy-to-do ideas to draw people of all ages together and help them to experience what it means to be part of a Christian community outside of Sunday worship. The book sets out the theory and practice of Messy Church and offers 15 themed programme ideas to get you started, each including Bible references and background, art and craft activities, recipes and family-friendly worship outlines.

'... crammed with good things... delights on every page... full of good fun, deep wisdom and practical know-how. Messy Church will be a blessing to many. I hope it leads to lots of mess and to many different forms of church.'
FROM THE FOREWORD BY THE RT REVD DR STEVEN CROFT

ISBN 978 1 84101 503 3   £8.99
Available from your local Christian bookshop or, in case of difficulty, direct from BRF using the order form on page 223.

ALSO BY LUCY MOORE

The Gospels Unplugged

52 poems and stories for creative writing, RE, drama and collective worship

This book is for busy church leaders and teachers who have endless demands on their time and energy and need stories that jump off the page, into the imagination and, from there, into daily life.

Drawn from all four Gospels, the pieces are 'unplugged' in that they get into the heart of the biblical text, reflecting the life of Jesus in action: who he is, what he said and what he did. Some tell the story, some explore an aspect of the original account. Many pieces include children.

Each piece comes with a short introduction of open-ended questions to encourage further exploration of the original story and the relevant Bible passage for reference. Some pieces are meant to be performed, some to be enjoyed quietly; but the overall aim is to have fun and enjoy unplugging the Gospels!

Includes photocopy permission.

ISBN 978 1 84101 243 8   £12.99
Available from your local Christian bookshop or, in case of difficulty, direct from BRF using the order form on page 223.